FOREIGN SERVICE FAMILY STYLE

A NARC TREADS AMONG THE DIPLOMATS

Ella Mae   Gordon

ELLA MAE RAYNER

GORDON J. RAYNER

Table of Contents

Maps for the areas in which we traveled

Paraguay

Ecuador

Uruguay

Bolivia

Argentina

Acknowledgments

We wish to thank The Writers Group at the Savannah Senior Center led by Bess Chappas. Over the past three years this group of experienced writers has helped us to develop our skills as novel writers.

Prior to this we were very good at writing reports and educational articles. With prodding, good natured corrections and constructive criticism we have produced this memoir.

We also thank our neighbors Marjorie and Leslie Dessauer for their time spent reviewing our work and supplying the final critique.

Polonius speaks . . . .

"This above all: To thine own self be true"

Hamlet, Act I, Scene 3

Prologue One

For the last 58 years I have dutifully listened to my husband repeat his war stories about the Marine Corps, the Border Patrol and the Drug Enforcement Agency. I finally realized I had some war stories of my own to tell.

While following Gordon through most of the Western hemisphere, I came upon many unusual and memorable people. I also had contacts with many cultures, which were not always easy but interesting and very memorable.

As I began to gather my thoughts to tell my tales, I soon realized his war stories would be a great contrast to my unexpected and sometimes bizarre encounters on the home front, wherever our home was at the time. I sat down and made an outline of Gordon's war stories and also my wild encounters. Thus came about the idea of two books or two stories told side by side.

As he moved forward from Marine Corps Sergeant through being a U. S. Border Patrol agent chasing wetbacks to a Federal Narcotics Agent serving as an Attaché with the US Embassy in Paraguay, his responsibilities grew, his work hours became erratic and at times his work took on a sinister flair.

Each new job required a move to another city, state or country. As his circumstances changed so did the structure of life within the family. As we adapted to the changes, our family became a cohesive unit and wherever Gordon went, the kids and I and sometimes cat went with him or followed closely in his wake. Throughout our lives his job was a family affair.

As you read the book, you will read about the hair rising adventures of a Narcotics agent, who does undercover work and is breaking new ground in a foreign country, along with what the family is doing at the same time.

Most of the chapters are written by one of us but several others are written as a joint effort because the events were shared.

Ella Mae Rayner

Prologue Two

Throughout the years, Ella Mae and I have kicked around the idea of writing about our adventures. Due to various other obligations, it was just a nebulous idea until about three years ago. One evening, while sitting on our verandah enjoying happy hour, the subject again arose and has now became a reality.

All of the events and situations described herein are factual and are from our memories of what we lived through. Some of the names have been changed to protect the innocent, but mostly to save the author from a punch in the nose.

Three years after I joined FBN, I was assigned to Operation Eagle in Miami, FL, in January of 1970. What started out as a one month assignment quickly turned into a six month tour. The end of January I flew back to Michigan to testify at a trial and by the end of my week of testimony my wife had decided, since I was in Miami and she and the kids were suffering from a severe winter in Detroit they were going to accompany me back to Miami for the season. She had the family packed, the house ready to be closed up and what seemed like all of our possessions packed into the travel trailer ready to drive to Miami. This included the Siamese cat and the kids' school records.

By mid June I had been selected to become the Special Agent In Charge, the Country Attaché, in Santiago, Chile. I was advised by BNDD Hdq. that the transfer, though not approved by the State Department, would be forthcoming. So, rather than restart our lives in Detroit for a short time, we would sell the house, ship the household goods to Chile and Ella Mae and kids would stay in Pennsylvania with her parents until the word of our move came. This was all done with BNDD Hdq approval.

After the house was sold and our furniture was shipped, we went for a visit with the in-laws in Pennsylvania. While there I was called to Headquarters in DC and found out that the government believed that Salvador Allende, a socialist/communist, was probably going to be elected President of Chile even though the US was actively trying to destabilize the Chilean elections to ensure that he was not elected.

Despite our government's overt and covert efforts, Allende was elected President of Chile and served until his assassination in September 1973. So we spent the next 7 months in limbo with the family in Pennsylvania and me TDY in Mexico City and Panama. Anticipating a move to somewhere in South America, the family did join me in Panama for Thanksgiving. Three months later we joined our furniture in New Orleans for a nine months' stay.

In March 1971, Auguste Ricord, "El Contrabandista," who had been a major player in the Sarte French Connection heroin smuggling operation since the early 1960s was placed under house arrest in Asuncion, Paraguay. His arrest was based on a warrant issued by the Eastern District of New York charging him with conspiracy to smuggle 42 kilograms of heroin which were seized in Miami in October 1970 in the Bianchi case. Informants and cooperating defendants in this Bianchi case identified Ricord as being one of the kingpins in the venture.

The only problem was that the government of President Alfredo Stroessner was dragging its feet in authorizing the extradition of Ricord to the United States for trial. Whether this hesitation was due to government corruption or the fact that smuggling was a way of life in Paraguay still is not known.

The brother-in-law of President Stroessner was in the business of importing liquor, cigarettes and small electronics from Panama by air. The planes would land in airfields close to the Argentine and Brazilian borders. Upon paying a transit tax to the government they would sell the goods to pilots who would legally export the items from Paraguay and in turn smuggle them into Argentina and Brazil where there were heavy import duties sometimes as high as 100% on luxury items.

At this time Paraguay had a very minimal drug abuse problem with only small amounts of local marijuana being consumed by the indigenous natives. There was no Paraguayan drug enforcement agency and only sketchy laws concerning legal drugs. Even the legal morphine based narcotics were not kept in a secure location at the local pharmacies as all medications could be purchased without a prescription. It was an almost idyllic society with the intoxicant of choice being the local liquor, Caña, and the only crimes against persons were when the natives got drunk and chopped at each other with their machetes on a Saturday night after partying at the local cantina.

The United States finally decided that some action was necessary to get the Paraguayan government to move forward with Ricord's extradition. Under the guise of assisting in the formation of and the training of a Paraguayan narcotics enforcement agency, as well as helping them update their old Napoleonic Code of drug laws, the government agreed that the United States should establish the office of Narcotics Attaché in the American Embassy in Asuncion. The main purpose was to have a presence on site to push for Ricord's extradition; ergo I was chosen to establish that office

Gordon J. Rayner

Chapter 1

On The Job

Here it is 2:00 AM on the 2nd night of a twenty four hour a day surveillance waiting for a load of heroin from Texas to be delivered to a stash house on Howard Street, here in Detroit, and still no sign of any activity. Tom, my senior partner, called on the radio and asked if there was anything happening.

I said, "No, even the hookers have called it a night and those two winos have both crashed in their cardboard box, in the alley over by the school. You know; the alley that has all of those rats that look as big as cats. It's a wonder that more of those winos don't get carried off by those critters."

"OK." Tom said "I'm going to stop at the Waffle House and grab a bite to eat. You want anything?"

"No thanks." I responded, "Just another cup of coffee to keep me awake. You know, *junkie style,* with lots of sugar and cream."

Tom said, "10-4. I'll be back in a flash."

I started thinking, Here I am on my first year's anniversary of being a Federal Narcotics Agent and I'm sitting in the middle of the Detroit ghetto at 2:00 AM, long stringy hair, a straggly mustache and wearing a ripped, dirty UAW warm-up jacket and a Detroit Tigers baseball cap. The funny thing is I am enjoying it. Boy, have I changed."

I laughed to myself as I remembered how I was dressed when I had first reported to the office to start the job, white sidewall haircut, a new three piece suit, white shirt, power tie and spit shined shoes. Hell, I think I was wearing a new pair of socks. What a change.

In 1967 after six years of chasing illegal aliens in Laredo, Texas, and Detroit, Michigan, I decided that I needed more excitement in life and took the Treasury Enforcement Agent (TEA) examination, which I passed and was put on the list of available applicants. The agencies that drew from this list included the US Customs Service, US Secret Service and the Federal Bureau of Narcotics. Within two months I had a successful interview with the Federal Bureau of Narcotics and became a Federal Narcotics agent.

This had thrown an entirely different light on my daily routine, the hours I worked, the time I would be home, the evenings or the weekends I needed to work and how much would I see of my family.

The day I joined the Federal Bureau of Narcotics (FBN) started with my arrival at the Federal building in downtown Detroit at about 8:30 AM for my nine o'clock appointment. I was apprehensive, as I had no real idea of what a Narcotic agent really did. Perhaps it was similar to the FBI on TV who carried a Thompson submachine gun with a big drum magazine, chasing bank robbers or kidnappers just like Elliot Ness.

About 8:45 AM two older women arrived and unlocked the office door and asked me what I wanted. I said, "I am the new hire and I am supposed to see the District Director (DD) at 9:00 o'clock."

Both of them laughed and said, "Go have breakfast and be back at about 10:00. That's the time the he usually gets in."

At 9:45 I was back on the bench outside the office pretending to read the newspaper but really watching the parade of characters going in the door down the hall from the main entrance to the office. First, there was a black guy with long dreadlocks, then a Mexican with Pachuco tattoos on both hands and his forehead, followed by a scraggly looking white guy with stringy hair and a grubby moustache. None were dressed in business suits or even sport coats and ties. They all looked like they had just come from the soup kitchen. *Who were these guys?*

Finally, the District Director, who had previously interviewed me, went by and entered the office without even glancing in my direction.

After about five minutes, the secretary came out and said, "He's ready for you now."

In we went and I was again introduced to the DD, who seemed to have forgotten ever meeting me previously. Brusquely, he called his deputy, Bill Thomas, into the office and had me raise my right hand and take the oath of office. He then handed me my new gold badge and told his deputy to take care of me.

Bill Thomas and I went across the hall to his office where he asked me what kind of law enforcement experience I had. When I told him of my seven years with the Border Patrol he broke out in laughter and called out, "Tom, get your sorry Mexican ass in here."

Through the door came the Mexican I had seen in the hallway. The deputy said "This guy is from the Border Patrol and is here to arrest you."

Tom looked at me and said, "Do you want to see my papelers?" I said in Spanish, "If you have them, then I can't arrest and deport you."

We all laughed as I had just been introduced to my new partner, who was to teach me how to be a good Narcotic agent.

My First Search Warrant

Two days later, several of us were sitting in a bar having a couple beers waiting for the evening rush hour to settle down, when Tom asked me if I had ever kicked in a door. I said "No, what the hell is that anyway?" He said, "Dummy, that's executing a search warrant." He then went to the telephone and came back and told me that we were going to assist the local drug squad in executing a search warrant that evening so I could '*get my feet wet.*'

About 8:00 PM that night we drove into a school parking lot and I was introduced to the sergeant and two other local narcotics agents. They said they had a search warrant for a house in the middle of the next block and that another team was covering the rear of the house and that we would be going in the front door. As I was the newbie, I would be the fourth man in the door and that I was to cover the stairs going to the second floor.

All was set with the other team in position in the back of the house. We parked at the corner and walked down the street to the address.

The sergeant said, "OK, Let's hit it"! We ran up on the porch with guns drawn.

The first man knocked on the door and yelled, "POLICE WITH A WARRANT!"

He stepped aside and the next officer kicked in the door lock. Bam! The door flew open and the first three ran to the right towards the main part of the house. I ducked to the left and looked up the stairs to the second floor. At the top of the stairs was a black dude with a gun in his hand.

I drew down on him, tightened the slack in the trigger and yelled "Police. You're a dead Mother.....!!!"

The next thing I knew he threw his gun in the air, dove to the floor and screamed "I'm a cop, don't shoot!"

When everything had settled down and my heart stopped racing, I found out that this officer was part of the back door coverage and had seen that there was an outside set of steps leading to the second floor. He went up the back steps, found the door was unlocked and entered the house just as we were coming through the front door.

From this I learned one thing and that was the seven P plan. Proper Prior Planning Prevents Piss Poor Performance. Also, when multiple agencies are involved in a raid situation, everybody meets everybody else and everyone knows what everybody is supposed to be doing.

A typical day of a Federal Narcotics "street" Agent would begin with arriving at the office at 9:00 AM for a brief team meeting to determine the general plans for the day. Did we have any urgent actionable information to work on, legal proceedings to take care of, and informants to contact or get out of jail; would we review ongoing cases or just wade through the ever present administrative paperwork that keeps the office running?

Then there were the daily tasks of contacting informants, planning further actions in ongoing investigations, preparing arrest warrants and search warrants and keeping up with prosecutions of those violators that had been arrested and were working their way through the judicial process. Hardly a day went by that what you had planned in the morning is what occurred for the whole day.

If an informant called and said a violator was expecting a delivery, it would be a mad rush to get surveillance agents on the street to document the fact or to arrange for an arrest and search and seizure of the drugs. Or, a prosecutor would call for help in responding to a defense motion on a pending case. Or, a local agency would call requesting help in a case that was going down that day.

Perhaps, there would be a meeting with the state or local drug units to go over ongoing joint investigations or to confer on future enforcement operations. Being the Feds, we usually had more resources to draw on and more money to spend than the locals, so our assets were always in demand. A brief visit to a local agency to have lunch could end up supporting them in an ongoing case, utilizing federal buy money, surveillance and undercover agents and backup for arresting defendants which meant I didn't get home until 3:00 AM.

Very few undercover buys went down as planned. We seldom could just walk in, buy the drugs and leave as in a grocery store, but it required chatting up the violator to convince him you were in the business, showing him the money and maybe just wait while he went to his source to get the drugs. Then you would make plans for future buys and attempt to obtain as much intelligence about the violator and his operation as possible.

Meanwhile before and during the buy, the surveillance agents would be obtaining information such as the violator's vehicles and license numbers, checking for counter-surveillance, making sure the deal wasn't a rip-off and identifying other customers of the dealer. Post-buy surveillance would also attempt to confirm any of the above facts.

Gosh, it is 4:00 AM and my shift as the eyeball is at an end. Here comes Tom to change places with me and I will take my turn at backup. I sure hope the agent, who is managing this case, calls his informant to make sure this is for real and not just a whore's dream.

Chapter 2

Family Life Evolves In A Narc's Household

Oh my gosh, here comes daddy. Does that mean we can't go?"

I and the three children were going out the back door with great plans to see a movie. We had done all the chores and together had picked out the movie we wanted to see. I really didn't want to put our plans on hold again.

Gordon and I had been high school sweethearts. After high school he went off to the Marine Corps and I started my nursing career at The Reading Hospital School of Nursing. After fourteen years of marriage and three children we were living in St Claire Shores, Michigan, when Gordon began to work for the Federal Bureau of Narcotics (FBN). I thought life as the wife of a border patrol agent was hectic, but I soon found out, life with a Narc was all together different.

As a border patrol agent he worked long hours and had several one or two week tours which took him away from home and I had begun to shoulder much of the family responsibility. As a Narc, his working hours were unpredictable to say the least. Sometimes he would just call and say, "I am headed out of town and I don't know when I will be back. I will buy clothes and the things I need when I get to where I am going, or I'm going out of town and I will be back in three." That could mean three hours, three days, three weeks, or three months.

There was no hint as to what he was doing or where he was going to be. I would just have to wait until he got back and he could share his exploits with me and I would bring him up to date on what the family had been doing. During happy hour he would tell me all about his trip, who he met, what happened to the bad guy, who he worked with and how he felt about what he was doing. I would tell him about my work at the hospital, what book the children and I were reading during the lunch hour, which of the children had gotten into trouble and what punishments had been doled out and any good things they had accomplished while he was gone.

Often the children would come home from school and I would say, "Guess what, Daddy is out of town and we can have liver and onions or tuna casserole. Which would you like tonight?"

Gordon wouldn't eat either of these meals, so we pigged out on them when he was gone.

The first household rule developed concerned the dinner hour. Dinner was a 6:00 PM. The children and I would eat at that time and I would keep a plate of food warm until 7:00 PM. If he could not be home by 7:00 PM he was to eat out or forage for himself when he came home. Because I was usually working as a nurse at one of the Detroit hospitals, I felt the household had to maintain some kind of routine for a bit of stability.

As time went along the family became used to his unscheduled absences. While he was gone we would plan our life around the four of us. There were movies to go to, school functions to attend, JC affairs to attend, church picnics and swim lessons. Usually when he did arrive home we would drop our plans and the family again centered on him. Today we were going out the door to see a movie which we wanted to see.

We were all very disappointed and the children stood around with long faces whispering to each other, "Why can't we go? We won't be gone long. Ah, gee, we are going to miss it."

That was the time I decided we were going to the movie. I said, "Dear, you can come with us or have a drink and a few quiet hours till we get back."

The discussion that evening at happy hour was about a new family rule. The way I saw it the children and I made up one social circle and Gordon, his partners and FBN were another social circle. When his circle intersected our household circle he would have to decide if and when to become part of ours. We would not drop what we were doing but he could take part in our plans at any time. These rules worked and kept out family stable through the years as our children were growing up.

Chapter 3

Strangers In A Far Distant Land

Paraguay is a land locked country bordered by the countries of Bolivia to the northwest, Brazil to the east and Argentina to the west and south. It is sub-tropical in nature and its border with Brazil is the Rio Parana and the border with Argentina is the Rio Paraguay. These two rivers flow southeast and eventually form the Rio de Plata which divides Argentina and Uruguay.

The only major city is the capital, Asuncion, on the western border with Argentina. In 1970 the only paved roads were in the capital and with one paved highway to Pilar, a city south of Asuncion on the Rio Paraguay. The main road from Pedro Juan Caballero on the border with Brazil was a dry weather road which was impassable in rainy weather, though it was the primary artery for goods coming from Brazil via heavy truck.

Commerce from the outside world had to be offloaded from ocean going freighters in Buenos Aires, Argentina, and loaded onto small riverine freighters which plied their way up the river to Asuncion or by trucks which had to be ferried across the Rio Paraguay at Pilar.

The paved road from the city ran a few miles past the international airport towards the Bolivian border. At that point the trucks were ferried across the Rio Paraguay to take a dirt road into the Chaco area several hundred kilometers into the Bolivian countryside.

Even though I had spent part of my childhood in Panama and my wife was reared on a farm in Lancaster County, Pennsylvania, I don't think we were ready for the culture shock of being in a third world country.

In Asuncion we had dependable electric power, telephones, trolley cars and a modern water system thanks to a USAID program in the early 1960s, but most of our calls back to relatives in the US were accomplished via ham radio operators. In fact, during my two year tour of duty in Asuncion, I received only two telephone calls from Headquarters in Washington, DC and one of those was a wrong number.

Air travel from the US was accomplished by the twice weekly Braniff flights from Miami via Panama, Guayaquil, Lima, La Paz, Asuncion and terminating in Buenos Aires on Sundays and Thursdays and return flights on Mondays and Fridays. Within Paraguay, the Aerolineas Paraguaya (LAP) used DC-3s to fly to the other cities on a daily basis. There were also twice weekly flights by LAP to Buenos Aires and Sao Paulo where you could connect with flights to Miami.

One time I was working with the Bolivian National Police (BNP) on an undercover deal in Cochabamba, and I had received death threats that the BNP thought were serious and advised me to get out of the country as soon as possible. As I arrived at the La Paz airport I could see the Braniff flight to Asuncion clearing the runway.

The only way I got out of town was to first fly from La Paz to Santiago via Iberia Airline to Montevideo via Lufthansa; to Buenos Aires via Aerolineas Argentina and finally Asuncion via LAP. Thank God for GTRs, the Official Airlines Guide and two passports.

Chapter 4

First Christmas in Paraguay

It was 1972 a few weeks before Christmas when we arrived at our first foreign post, Asuncion, Paraguay. My husband, Gordon, I and our three children, Georgie Anne 15, Gregory age 9 and Jo age 8, flew in on the bi-weekly Braniff flight from Miami.

This particular Braniff 707 had a bright colorful exterior that had been designed by the artist, Andrew Calder. We were embarking on our first adventure of family living in a Latin American country and everyone was excited. We were met by an Embassy representative, given a map of the area, told of the trolley routes and the train routes and then deposited at a pension.

The first week or two we spent at the pension (a small inn or hotel) because there were no motels in Paraguay and only one large triangular shaped hotel in downtown Asuncion. This pension was surrounded by many colorful tropical plants the outstanding of which were the frangipani trees. These trees were six to seven feet tall and umbrella shaped; in Paraguay their flowers were red with bits of white. The green plants throughout the garden were shades of dark green. The major leaves were one to two feet wide and hung heavily to the ground.

A soft breeze was flowing through the open windows and doors of a one story sandstone building which was the office and main dining room for the pension. Ten or twelve small outlying buildings also made of sandstone were the apartments or living quarters. The bathrooms within the apartments had a wash bowl and toilet but the shower was located about ten feet out-side the apartment. Since there was no hot water, no one lingered long in the shower. In South America the seasons are reversed therefore we were thankful it was the beginning of summer.

Before coming to Paraguay, the whole family had studied Spanish. Georgie had enrolled in a high school Spanish class and I had permission to audit the class. We read several histories of the country and I developed a fun way for Greg and Jo to learn the language and the geography of South America. A large piece of brown wrapping paper was placed on the kitchen table and on it was drawn a map of South America and Paraguay. The mountains, rivers, flora and fauna of the area were drawn and named in both English and Spanish. We learned Paraguay and its neighbor Bolivia were the two poorest and underdeveloped countries in South America and were the two countries with no coastline. Paraguay had only two paved roads and the inhabitants were a mix of Germans, Spaniards and local Guaraní Indians. Languages spoken were Spanish and a local language called Guaraní.

The week before Christmas, we moved into a house a few blocks from the Embassy. As per usual, my husband deposited the family at the new house, and went on detail out of town, thus leaving the family to take care of settling into our new surroundings. Before he left he did take care of hiring our maid, Vicky. Thank goodness. She could at least give us some help with finding our way around this new city and culture. My Spanish was not the greatest but we could communicate.

Vicky appeared for her interview in blue shaded sunglasses, was five foot three, a bit on the plump side and about 45 years old. She had short dark brown hair with a bit of a curl, had a ruddy complexion and was slow to smile After she was settled into her little room at the back of the house, Gordon shared an embarrassing moment he had during the interview with Vicky.

Besides asking about the pay rate, she asked, "Es el trabajo con costumbre?"

His knowledge of Spanish did not include this idiom and he asked her to explain. She used another more direct Spanish term to ask if she was obligated to sleep with the master of the house. He quickly said no and she accepted the position.

Our new abode was a sprawling house with large tiled floors throughout. A massive stone fireplace took up 1/3 of the living room wall; to the rear of the house were the children's rooms and the kitchen. Beyond the house was a large closed in back yard and open patio. This was all surrounded by a 4 foot sandstone wall with bits of colorful broken glass imbedded across the top. A sturdy gate provided access for the car and a smaller gate led to the walk and the front door. We were all a bit speechless as home had never been so spacious.

The furniture and appliances supplied by the embassy slowly arrived and were installed in their proper places. My goal was to have the home set up and running by the time Gordon returned for Christmas. Once the house was in order I went looking for Christmas decorations.

The meat and produce markets were all open air except for the one small German market that had refrigeration. The stores down town reminded me of pictures of the western towns in America in the early 1900s. They were two story wooden buildings unpainted and with high windows. Sale items were a mixture of hardware, dress material, house wares, second-rate locally made handicrafts, jewelry, hand embroidered pictures and clothes.

I looked through many of them and found no Christmas decorations. I was finally told here in Paraguay they do not celebrate Christmas, but do celebrate the coming of the Christ child on Epiphany which is the first week in January. Well that was not going to do it for me. Being in a new country I had to have something of the old culture to hang on to, not only for the children but for my husband and myself.

I found a few decals that had a hint of Christmas to stick on the windows as well as a few green and red garlands to hang from the fireplace. Then I resorted to good Old Dutch Cleanser which I liquefied and drew pictures of snow, candles, holly wreaths and angels on the windows. Alas, there would be no Christmas tree or Santa Claus this year.

I discovered an English speaking United Christian church for us to attend on Christmas Eve. In Asuncion, Paraguay, united meant a union of all the English speaking believers in the area. There were Anglicans, Lutherans, Pentecostals, Baptists, Christian Scientists and Catholics who attended. There were also Mormons in Asuncion but they had their own church in which to worship. In order to accommodate all these religious sects, each Sunday the pulpit was filled by a pastor or layman of a different faith.

The Catholic priest, who was five foot three and quite rotund, proclaimed from the pulpit, "Of all the volunteer clergy, I believe I fill this pulpit the best."

My husband arrived home the day before Christmas. Vicky and I had bought a lomito (a filet mignon cut of beef), potatoes and fresh green beans and I had made a pumpkin pie. Gordon had brought home some wine and champagne to add to the festivities. As we sat down to our dinner we realized this was not a Christmas to compare to any Christmas past, but we were together as a family and as a family we were ready to face the world and experience the interesting adventures which lay ahead.

Chapter 5

Extradition Bolivian Style

After I arrived in Paraguay, I learned my area of responsibility would include Bolivia. Its capital, La Paz, was located on the slope of a mountain dropping from the Altiplano, a flat high desert plain which encompassed several hundred square miles at 11,000 feet with the central business area being located down the slope at about 9,000 feet.

Until one got acclimated to the altitude and the body built up more blood to carry oxygen to the brain, one would suffer short term memory loss. This could be embarrassing if, half way through a conversation, you forgot what you were talking about. Most of the personnel in the Embassy wrote down everything you talked about in the government's standard little green book. I thought this was silly, until one day I was writing a report and needed some information from a guy down the hall.

I walked to his office and said, "Hello ......" I realized I had forgotten what it was I wanted.

Two months after arriving in Asuncion I received an urgent cable from the regional office in Buenos Aires.

"Agent Rayner, go to La Paz ASAP. Meet with the CIA station chief to expedite the removal of a DEA fugitive who is being held by the Bolivians on an immigration charge. Use any means necessary to get him to the Panama Canal Zone where the US has jurisdiction to arrest him."

When I got to La Paz, I met with the CIA station chief and we went to the office of the General in Charge of the Bolivian National Police. He was a middle aged well built gentleman dressed in faultlessly tailored khakis, spit shined cavalry boots and a glossy Sam Browne belt. He rose from his chair to shake our hands and with great flourish served us Bolivian espresso café which was strong, syrupy and sweet. After an hour of small talk about friendship, international cooperation and other bullshit, we decided the easiest way get the fugitive to the Canal Zone was to load him on a US Air Force C- 141 that was delivering military supplies to the Bolivians the next day.

As we were leaving the office, the General said, "Oh, by the way. I'll send my adjutant to guard the prisoner until we can turn him over to the US officials in the Canal Zone. I'm sure you will arrange to have an escort officer to meet my adjutant and stay with him until he is done in the base PX. There are a few things I want him to pick up."

I readily agreed with this and was again ready to leave his office.

Once more he said, "Oh, by the way. It would be nice of the DEA to provide me with a gesture of international goodwill. Since I am an admirer of Smith and Wesson revolvers, could you arrange to get me about 10 or 12 of them?"

I said, "Yes sir, I will see if that can be done."

"Oh, by the way that will be with a case of ammunition won't it?"

What could I say? Finally we were able to leave his office before I gave away the whole store. The CIA station chief thought it was hilarious. I had no idea how I was going to get him the guns but at least the fugitive would be in US custody.

When we got back to the Embassy, I finally got to read a copy of the arrest warrant and found out the fugitive Juan Carlos Apiro (alias) was a well documented member of the French Connection who was involved in the smuggling of several loads of heroin into New York. "Oh crap, if this guy is such a heavy weight, maybe the syndicate may try to free him on the way to the airport?"

The next morning, two CIA Agents and I showed up at the General's office in a GMC carry-all to pick up the fugitive and the adjutant for the long drive through the city up to the airport on the Altiplano. As we drove through the workers' section of town a large truck pulled out in front of us and blocked the road.

In a heartbeat the one CIA Agent had an Uzi in his hands and the driver and I both had our automatics in our hands as I screamed to the fugitive "You're the first one to die!"

It was a false alarm.

When we arrived at the cargo terminal at the La Paz airport, our aircraft was ready to take us to the Canal Zone. Several hours later we landed at Howard Air Field and were met by the DEA Agent In Charge, Bill Plase and a US Marshal, who formally arrested Apiro and who would take Apiro before the US Magistrate the next afternoon for his initial appearance.

After the US Marshal took away the prisoner, I told Bill, "I could seriously stand a drink."

"We can get a drink at my house. Why don't you stay at my house? The hearing tomorrow won't be until eleven o'clock. That would be easier than having to drive you to the hotel and returning to bring you back to the Zone."

"That's a great idea."

Since Bill was an old friend and we hadn't seen each other in a while, one drink led to another and we finally crashed about 4 AM. The next thing I knew, it was 7:00 AM and Bill's wife was shaking me awake telling me, "The Panama Canal Zone Governor's office just called and demanded that you and Bill be in his office at eight o'clock to explain what you did yesterday without getting his approval."

As I was staggering around with a major hangover trying to get dressed, I realized our government and the Panamanian government were in negotiations about transferring the Canal Zone back over to Panama and they did not want such an overt exercise of US governmental authority. So at eight o'clock sharp, Bill and I, both looking like death warmed over, were in the governor's office. Fortunately, the secretary had mercy on us and gave us a cup of coffee and then another.

Boy was the Governor pissed!! He didn't care who the prisoner was or what he had done. It was NOT acceptable. Unfortunately, it was a *fait accompli* and we damn sure weren't going to un-arrest our defendant.

The Governor pounded his fist on the desk and said, "I will fire both of you and put you in jail."

Bill and I had enough of his pompous performance and between the two of us told him we did not work for him and we were accredited diplomats to our host country governments and the operation had been approved by the Department of Justice and the Department of State. He then calmed down a little bit and we were able to get out of his office.

As we were walking back to the car, I turned to Bill and said, "Well, at least he can't declare you Persona Non Grata (PNG)." We laughed as neither of us knew that we would be declared Persona Non Grata within the new few years. The government of Panama declared Bill and the other two DEA agents in his office Persona Non Grata because DEA was investigating the brother of the President of Panama on drug smuggling charges. Also two years later the US Ambassador in Paraguay would declare me persona Non Grata because I did not follow his orders to the letter.

After we left the Governor's office, Bill and I went to Bill's office in Panama City where I called Jerry Strickland, the Latin American Controller in Headquarters, to fill him in on what had transpired. Jerry was full of praise for what we had done until I told him, "Oh by the way, it will cost us twelve Smith and Wesson revolvers and a case of ammunition for the Bolivian General of Police."

He groaned and replied, "Don't you know there is a law against supplying arms to foreign governments?"

My stomach churned. "Now is a good time to tell me. The General was very happy about the deal and if we renege, I don't think the Bolivians are going to trust us in the future."

There was silence from the other end then Jerry said, "I'll see what I can do, but just don't put anything in a cable or in a report that mentions the guns or there could be lots of heat from the suits or the politicians if they find out."

About three months later, I got another vague cable from headquarters saying the supplies I had ordered had arrived and I should fly to La Paz and pick them up. Two days later, I flew to La Paz and went to the Embassy and met with the CIA station chief.

He looked over his eyeglasses and said, "I don't know what you are talking about. You must have me confused with the Agency for International Development (AID) chief. He sometimes receives stuff that he turns over to the Bolivians. I know we don't"

I said, "Oh yeah, you're right. It must be the altitude getting to me. You know the lack of oxygen in the air."

Out the door I went and down to the AID office where the chief, Jose Cuervo (alias), closed his office door and then unlocked a closet. There sitting on the floor were the twelve Smith & Wessons and the case of ammunition. I then spent several hours recording the descriptions and serial numbers of the guns. I had worked for the government for too long and I was damned if I was going to turn them over to the General without some sort of receipt. *Maybe. Just a scribbled hand written piece of paper, but something.*

The next morning, Cuervo and I, carrying two packages wrapped in cheap brown paper, drove to the General's office where we were admitted, each of us carrying a package.

The General, dressed in his usual attire, warmly greeted us and immediately started unpacking the guns. He reacted, like a kid on Christmas morning, as he gleefully examined each one.

When he was done, he said, "You are not like some of these CIA guys who promise a lot and don't give you crap. You kept your word and I am looking forward to working with DEA."

I handed him the receipt to sign which he did with a flourish, handing me my copy and calmly throwing his copy in the trash.

Chapter 6

Summer Camp In January

Christmas was over, January had arrived and it was still summer. I was having a hard time adjusting to living in the southern hemisphere where the seasons are reversed. The children really enjoyed it, "No school for another three months." Of course my husband was again traveling all over South America making his contacts in the Embassies of the other countries. This left the children and me free to explore.

We became involved with the United Christian church group and made new friends among several of the missionaries in the area. My daughter, Georgie, became a life guard at the American Embassy pool and Greg and Jo, who were regular fish when there was any water to dive into, were now part of the American Embassy swim team.

About three weeks into this routine, a member of the Baptist Church group approached me to ask a *big favor*.

"I hear you are an RN. Our summer camp is in dire need of a nurse and if we have no nurse, there will be no summer camp for our kids."

"Well, yes, tell me about it."

"The camp site is a primitive one and is one hour out of town by bus. We can't pay you because the missionary group has very little money. What is collected is used for food and supplies. The camp lasts two weeks, Monday through Friday, and we will be coming home the weekend in between. The first week is for children age six to twelve and the second week is for children age thirteen and above. There is a charge of $20.00 per child but you can take your three children free."

"That's fine but I will not leave any child behind while I am at camp. If I can take the three children both weeks, I'm your nurse."

The camp personnel agreed and we all got ready to go to camp. The children needed bathing suits, clothes for five days, towel and washcloth, bar of soap, bed clothes, bug spray, sunscreen and toiletries. As the camp nurse I put together a few items from my family medical supplies. Band-aids and adhesive tape topped the list along with mercurochrome, rubbing alcohol, hydrogen peroxide and antibiotic ointment to treat cuts, a sling for possible broken arms, an ace bandage for sprains and a few tongue blades in case anyone was epileptic.

Of course Gordon wasn't home and I didn't know when he would return. We just left a note telling him we were at camp and would be back at the end of the week. We also included a map in case he came home early and wanted to join us.

The bus we took to camp was a bit old and rickety and carried about 30 children and counselors. The back bumper was rusty and hung to one side. The sides lacked paint and had a bit of rust here and there and the motor ran a bit rough. In Paraguay no one cared about a bit of rust or the condition of the motor. As long as the bus moved and got us to camp, everything was OK.

The counselors kept the children amused singing songs such as "Kumbaya," "Michael, Row Your Boat Ashore," "You can't get to Heaven on Roller Skates" and "Deep & Wide." Everyone was grinning from ear to ear just anticipating the fun they would have at camp. After an hour of singing, jostling, laughing and telling stories we arrived at the camp site.

Our family had spent several vacations in primitive camp sites, but what I saw did not compare in any way. The camp site was a fourteen acre, mostly wooded area. There was a clearing in the center which was covered with dead leaves and small branches. At one end was an open pavilion with fourteen or more grimy picnic tables stacked inside of it. At the far end of the pavilion was a wood-burning stove with four burners and a stone sink (the dish washing area) that needed a good cleaning. The sink reminded me of the horse troughs we had on my father's farm but they were cleaner than this one. To the left of the camp site were small cabins and two bath houses, one for the boys and one for the girls. The cabins were sparsely furnished with two bunk beds and two bedside stands

Finally, I went looking for the swimming pool. I could hear all the shouting and splashing, so I just followed the noise.

My mouth dropped open, *I can't believe this! No way should the children be swimming in this.*

The pool was Olympic size with a few lane dividers strung from end to end. The water was brownish black in color and I could see no more than five inches into the water. Running on the lane dividers were several huge water bugs. I had seen water bugs before at the Embassy pool, but these were quarter to half dollar in size and their shield shaped backs glistened in the sun as they run up the dividers.

I could not imagine why the pool was in this condition. I checked to see how the water was supplied to the pool and found a spring about fifty feet away. With continuous spring water the pool should have been cleaner.

I questioning a local caretaker who told me, "I put chemicals into the pool like I was told. No one tell me to do anything else to the pool."

I checked the pool more closely and noticed the three inch outlet pipe at one end was capped. I unscrewed the cap and laid it to the side and watched as some of the crud went flowing downstream. When I checked the pool the next day, I found someone, probably the caretaker, had recapped the outlet. I took care of the problem. I kept the cap in my room for the two weeks we were in camp and by the time we left I could see about five feet into the water thanks to the splashing kids and the constant flow through of water.

First on my agenda was to clean up the stone sink. The camp managers had brought cleaning supplies which thankfully included bleach, brushes and rags. After an hour and a lot of elbow grease the sink was at an acceptable standard of cleanliness. Another area that drew my attention was the ice box. There was no refrigerator here, just an old insulated box for a block of ice. After another half hour of scrubbing, I declared it was ready for food storage.

Food in this new land of ours was also what you might call primitive. No fast foods here. Because there was no electricity for refrigeration, food was bought daily at the <u>open fresh market</u>. Fresh pineapples, potatoes, cabbages and any other seasonal items were piled on a table or on the side of the street. Burlap bags or straw under the vegetables were optional. Steers, goats, or pigs were slaughtered daily and very early in the morning and hung up in the market. Your order was sliced directly from the carcass and wrapped in newspaper for you to carry home. To ensure you had fresh meat you needed to shop early before the hot sun hit the fresh kill. Poultry was mostly sold live, or as you might say, on the wing.

The camp managers had hired a Paraguayan cook for these two weeks. She was more adept at buying and cooking under these conditions. The thing I was most concerned about was her lack of interest in cleanliness. I thought to myself, *I will have to keep a close eye on her.*

I was surprised I had no big medical problems to treat. These children seemed to be a hail and hardy bunch. My only patient was an older child with a case of conjunctivitis which developed the second day of camp and I was going to send him home.

He pleaded and begged, "Don't send me home, my mom won't let me come back."

"I'll see what I can do." I didn't want to disappoint this child, so I decided to check out the local farmacia (pharmacy). In Paraguay no one needed a prescription to buy drugs, just money.

As I searched for a boric acid powder to make a weak solution to wash out the eyes, I found many name brand antibiotics, salves of all kinds and bug sprays. Of course everything was written in Spanish. I finally found the boric acid powder and to my surprise the outside of the box contained the directions to make a mild solution. Back I went to my primitive kitchen where I boiled water to sterilize the small container and the equipment I would need to mix the solution which I would use to cleanse the eyes of this scared child. It worked! He stayed the rest of the week to splash in the pool and play with the rest of the children.

One morning, during the second week of camp, I got up early and was met by an overwhelming putrid odor coming from the kitchen area, especially the ice box.

I woke up the camp manager and said, "I think the piece of meat we bought yesterday has turned bad. We need to get rid of it before everyone gets up."

We quietly removed the rancid meat from the ice box, wrapped it in a burlap bag and buried it behind the pavilion. After a thorough scrubbing the odor was gone, thank goodness. However, that was not the end of the story. I heard a day later the Paraguayan cook had dug up the rancid meat and taken it home. Because meat in their home was a rarity, she washed the meat, cut off and threw away the affected parts and fed what was left to her family.

The children and I had a nice surprise on the last day of camp. About mid day a shinny blue car came slowly up the lane and who got out of the car but Gordon. We ran to greet him as he was our super hero. He arrived home from his travels around South American and had followed the directions we left for him. He spent the last night at camp with us. The next morning as everyone was getting on the bus and waving good-by, our family got to drive home together in the air conditioned car.

Chapter 7

Reader's Digest Contact

Prior to my arrival in Paraguay, August Ricord, El contrabandista, had been indicted in Federal court in NYC on charges he had smuggled over 100 kilos of French heroin through Paraguay to the United States. The Paraguayan officials had detained him and placed him under house arrest, but were dragging their feet on extraditing him to the US. This situation persisted despite our efforts to get the Paraguayan government to move on this issue.

Then, about two months after I reported to Asuncion, I received a cable from Washington advising me Nate Adams, senior Editor for *Reader's Digest,* would be arriving in a week to gather information on the Ricord case for a feature length story he was writing and I was to afford Mr. Adams the utmost cooperation in his endeavors. I saw that the US consul's office was included as an action office on the cable. This was extremely unusual, so I picked up the phone and rang Gordon Garrett, the US Consul, whose office was on the first floor and asked him if he had a minute to discuss the cable we had both received.

Gordon said, "Of course, I'll be right up. You know my office is not secure with all of these locals coming in and out. It'll take me a few minutes, I have to open my safe to get my copies of the cable traffic I have on this."

Copies of his cable traffic. Hell, I had just gotten the one cable. What was going on?

When Gordon arrived in my outer office, he told my secretary to go have a coffee with her husband and he would let her know when she could come back. He then locked my outer office door, came into my office, closed the door, pulled down the venetian blinds, drew a large sealed manila envelope from under his coat and said, "OK, I think we can begin."

"Gordon" I said, "Why all the secrecy?"

"Well," he answered, "You know I was the local Embassy contact for BNDD before you arrived. It was supposed to be confidential and I don't want anyone here to find out what I was doing. I'm only supposed to be the Consul, not an undercover agent."

He then unsealed the envelope and handed me copies of the cable traffic he had with the State Department regarding Ricord. I was surprised to read a young Captain in the National Police had been the original source of information about Ricord and his activities in Paraguay.

It appeared the officer was the precinct commander in the area where Ricord had his restaurant and house and he had compiled a list of the important people who visited Ricord. This list included ranking government officials, business people, suspected smugglers and pilots, as well as unidentified French associates of Ricord.

I was miffed that I had not been given any of this information. Here I was in Asuncion and there was a good chance I would encounter many of these players, but no one had bothered to tell me about them. Such is life. The next Thursday I drove to the airport to pick up Mr. Adams when his Braniff flight arrived.

I parked my government car, walked into the main lobby and saw the flight would be a half hour late. Not an unusual occurrence. So, I went into the bar to have a beer to kill time. As I sat sipping my cold St. Pauli Girl beer, I felt a tap on my shoulder, turned around and found the Major, who was Director of the airport, smiling at me.

"Senor Rayner, what brings you out here today? Are you meeting someone or waiting for the air freight like the last time?"

"Hola Major. No, I won't pull that air freight thing again. I've learned to just ship everything through the diplomatic pouch or the APO mail, so your Customs doesn't charge me an arm and a leg in duties. That Christmas tree was the most expensive one I ever had. I can't understand why my dumb brother-in-law sent the thing by international air freight, collect!"

"So then you must be meeting someone. Is it another spy?"

"Come on Major. I'm not a spy, I'm a narcotics agent."

"So, who is it you're meeting?"

"Just an old friend on a business trip to Buenos Aires who decided to stop by for a visit since he was coming through Paraguay."

"Oh, Okay, have a nice day. I'll see you around."

"Well, they're watching me again. I hope I can recognize Adams."

The Braniff flight finally arrived and as the passengers were deplaning, I carefully checked them out to see if I could identify Adams. It was the easiest ID I had ever made. Most of the other passengers were Latinos and three of the four Anglos on the flight were being met by the local Mormons, who were calling out their praises to God. That left only one man it could possibly be; he looked exactly like I had pictured an Executive Editor of *Readers Digest*. He had longish hair, a well trimmed beard, horn rimmed glasses, a tweed jacket with leather elbow patches, khaki chinos and a camera and tape recorder slung over his shoulder.

After the passengers had cleared Immigration and were waiting for their luggage, I casually went over to the baggage claim area, walked up behind Adams and in a loud voice cried out, "Nate, it's good to see you again you old son of a gun!"

Surprised, Adams turned around and said, "You must be from the Embassy."

I nodded my head slightly, rolled my eyes and replied, "You don't even recognize your best friend? Hell it's only been six years. I haven't changed that much, have I?"

His eyes finally lit up and he said, "Jeez, you'll have to forgive me, it was a rough flight and I didn't get much sleep last night."

As the Mormons were the only ones around that understood English, I added,

"You gotta stop drinking that rot gut booze and stop smoking those cheap cigars. That will make anyone sick."

No one seemed to pay us any attention, and without another word, we picked up his bags and calmly walked out to my car. Once I had thrown his bags in the trunk, we both got into the car, where Adams said, "Golly, I didn't think it was going to be this bad!"

As I started the car, I said, "It's not you. Because I am the US Narcotics Attaché, every time I come to the airport to meet someone they check out who it is I am picking up. It's just a game that the Major and I play. Anyway, I made a reservation for you at the Pension Naccional, where everybody stays. It's clean, quiet, serves decent food and booze and is away from downtown and close enough for you to walk to the Embassy, if you want. Besides, you can always grab a taxi to go anywhere you want to go and the taxi drivers won't rip you off like in downtown."

"That sounds great, let me check in and I'll buy you a drink so we can talk."

"OK, but for the drinks, we can go to my house. Maybe you can charm my wife into inviting you to dinner too."

After Adams checked in and dropped his bags in his room, he came back to the car and we drove to my house for a few drinks and some serious conversation. I really wanted to know the who, what, where and how of the information he had gotten about Ricord as he appeared to have a hell of a lot more knowledge of it than I did.

At my house, as we started on our second Beefeaters on the rocks, Adams related that actually, *Readers Digest* had gotten a call from the State Department suggesting we may be interested in the case and perhaps would do a feature article on Ricord and the Paraguayan reluctance on his extradition. He said that when he visited the State Department they let him read through a thick file on Ricord which included all of the State cable traffic as well as the BNDD cable traffic and most of the BNDD case file. It was more than I had even dreamed the government would leak to a civilian entity. It was more than I knew existed or had been made aware of.

After dinner, I drove Adams back to the Pension Naccional, handed him my business card, gave him directions to the Embassy and said I would see him in the morning.

Early the next morning I arrived at the Embassy and found Adams waiting at the Marine Guard's desk. I said, "Geez, I didn't expect him until nine o'clock."

The Marine Guard snorted, "Hell, Mr. Rayner, he's been here for over a half hour."

As we walked to my office Nate laid out his plan of action.

"First, I want to talk to Gordon Garrett, the consul, and arrange an interview with his source that provided most of the information about Ricord. Then I want to talk with the Attorney General, Campos Alum, to get the government's take on this case. After I've talked to them, maybe I'll just wander around the city and do some one on one interviews with the people."

"Okay, first things first. Let me do the protocol thing and introduce you to the DCM, and then I'll call Gordon and have him come up here to meet with you. The second one is a little tougher, but I think we can arrange a meeting with Campos Alum. The Embassy will probably even provide you with an interpreter when you talk to him. The third one is up to you, I don't think it would be wise for me to go with you around the streets of downtown, but you can do it on your own."

After introducing Adams to the DCM, we returned to my office where we met with Garrett and it was arranged that he would contact the police officer about a meeting, but Garrett said it couldn't be at his house as he had a security guard at night and the guard reported all visitors to the Ministry of Interior (MI).

Garrett suggested we have the meeting at my house, as there was a back entrance and it would be easy to sneak in even if the MI was watching the front of the house. I readily agreed to this and about an hour later Garrett came back to my office, closed the door, pulled down the venetian blinds, took a seat with his back to the window.

In a low voice he said, "It is arranged for tomorrow evening. The officer and I will come in the back of your property. Leave the rear gate unlocked and don't shoot us when we arrived. I will knock twice rapidly, pause and then knock once on the back door so you will know who it is."

I managed to keep a straight face and agreed with the plan.

The next day I told Vicki, our maid, she could have the evening off and suggested that she go to the movies. She refused, saying it was not proper for a woman to go out at night alone.

"Okay, how about you go over to visit your sister?"

"Oh, Señor, if you are having a secret meeting or something, just tell me to stay in my room and I will."

"That will be great, but if you hear any shots being fired don't stick your head out the door until I or the Señora come for you."

"Si señor!"

Just after eight o'clock as Nate and I were sitting in the parlor, there was the agreed upon signal knock at the back door. With gun in hand, I slowly, unlocked the rear door and admitted Garrett and the police officer. As I was relocking the back door, Garrett rushed into the front room and, without even nodding to Adams, hurriedly closed the front drapes and turned off all of the lights.

I cried out, "Damn, Gordon, we have to have enough light to see each other. Sit the hell down and get a hold of yourself. I checked the street not ten minutes ago and everything is cool. Besides, you're scaring Nate as well as your guest."

"Okay, okay. I guess I am a little uptight, but I'm not used to doing this undercover stuff."

"Why don't you make the introductions, Gordon? Just relax and pretend we're in your office trying to get a visa or something."

Things finally calmed down and after the introductions, the Police Officer related to Adams, with Gordon translating, the story of his investigation of August Ricord, the infamous Latin Connection.

For the next several days, I saw and heard little from Adams, and then he burst into my office and said, "We have to go to Buenos Aires, there are some things I have to talk over with Frank."

"What's this we stuff? Hell, you can just jump on a plane and be there in no time."

"No, you don't understand, I called your Regional Director and he said that you have to come with me."

"Well, who am I not to do what the RD says to do. Donnie, call the travel office downstairs and have them get me a ticket to B.A. on tomorrow's flight, make a reservation for me and Adams and get my wife on the phone while I think up a good excuse for not taking her with me."

"After you are done that, will you please, send a cable to B.A. and advise them of our travel plans and have them make reservations at the Sheraton and tell Frank we will see him for lunch and that *Reader's Digest* will pay for it."

Chapter 8

Homes in Paraguay

Our first home in Paraguay was large and spacious. However, as summer turned to autumn, heavy rains began to fall and we learned our home had a rather large flaw. The large and beautiful fireplace which made up a major part of the living room became a waterfall.

The first small rainfall was no problem because only a few leaks appeared and they were wiped up with little trouble. Then came a gully washer; the water poured down the face of the fireplace. Vicky and I quickly moved the furniture and the one large rug to the high end of the living room. I had noticed the tile floor had a bit of a slant to the center of the room where there was a drain.

I thought to myself. *Now I know why that drain was* placed in *the middle of the living room.*

After two of these emergency drainage problems, we began to look for another place to live. Most of the embassy personnel lived in the American enclave. However, we felt very adventuresome and opted to live in a Paraguayan neighborhood. We heard of a house that would be available. Colonel Nesbitt, who belonged to the Mil Group and his family, would be moving in a few months. It was about a mile down the street from the Embassy and the President's palace. We couldn't wait to move to dryer ground.

When we finally moved into the big house, we believed we had moved to a mansion. The house was on a large corner lot and was completely surrounded by a six foot sandstone wall. A double iron gate provided entry to the driveway and a small iron gate opened to steps and the walk which led to the front door. If we had wanted to, we could have locked ourselves in or the local merchants and neighbors out.

The thing that surprised us most was the condition of the boulevard in front of the house. You have to remember we were only a few blocks from the President's home in the capital city of the country. There was a median for trees and flowers in which grew immature trees but no flowers. Instead there was tall grass and the median was surrounded by barbed wire. We were told that the cows and other animals roamed freely and would eat the flowers and the trees if there were no barbed wire.

Now to describe the mansion: The living room/dining room was as long as a bowling alley with a three sided fireplace close to one end. The floor consisted of large beige tiles and there were windows on three sides of the room. A rear door led to the kidney shaped swimming pool which was surrounded by large reddish brown tiles. The remaining wall and the walls of the rest of the mansion were two feet thick and finished with smooth plaster and cream colored enamel paint This room sure was bright, inviting and roomy.

As we walked to the rear of the house we passed through the daily dining room. Yes, the Paraguayans have two dining rooms, a formal dining room and the daily dining room. Something many Americans do not have. We may have a breakfast nook but not a large expanse of a room.

The daily dining room is used by the family at breakfast and lunch. The formal dining room is used for dinner by the older family members as children would eat in the daily dining room unless it was a special occasion. Of course the formal dining room is used to entertain guests, such as other family relatives, government officials and to host other social events. There is not much outside entertainment to be had and socializing is done in each others' homes.

The girls' large bedroom and bath were to the rear of the house. The bedroom was at least fourteen feet by fourteen feet and the windows faced the pool. Their bathroom had a seven foot sunken tiled tub with shower, a wash bowl, a toilet and a bidet. As the girls were fifteen and nine years old, there were a lot of giggles about the bidet. It ended up being used to shave their legs, wash swimsuits and sneakers as well as for what it was designed.

Next to the daily dining room was a medium sized kitchen with a gas stove, refrigerator, a nice sink with an ample prep area and many cabinets. There was cold running water but no hot water. I frequently walked into the kitchen to check the temperature of the water being used to wash the dishes as Vicky, the maid, would be washing dishes with cold water if I didn't check on her. There was a bath next to the daily dining room that housed a small gas hot water heater which supplied the other two baths.

Past the daily dining room was a large room about sixteen by sixteen with a door to the outside. It had been designed to be used for an office but I turned it into a library which became my pride and joy.

A large five foot round lapacho wood table was placed in the middle of the room and there were five foot high shelves on two walls. These I filled with monthly magazines, novels for all ages, reference books, maps, and games.

A stairway led up to the master bedroom and bath. For the size of the house the master bath was very small and contained a shower, small bowl and toilet. On the floor was a small gas heater which had to be lit every morning in order to heat the area. A door next to the bath led to an open air patio that was the roof of the living/dining room area. This area could be used for parties or to enjoy the starry evenings when weather permitted.

This mansion had no central heating. Asuncion, Paraguay, is located equal degrees south of the equator as Savannah is north. You can imagine how cold it can be as the weather in winter can become as cold there as in Savannah. In the winter the doors to the daily dining room were closed and the family did most of their living in the daily dining room as it was just off the kitchen and was heated with a movable gas heater. The girls would move the heater into their bathroom or bedrooms as needed. The three sided fireplace in the living room was put to good use and was kept going most of the time. Because the room was so large we huddled close to the fireplace in our sweat suits and blankets to read, talk or play games.

As you can tell this was a big house that needed a lot of care. This is why Paraguayan families have servants who live on premises. The servants' quarters were in an unattached small building situated twenty feet behind the mansion. It had one bedroom and bath with cold running water.

Within our walls was about an acre of vegetation. Two large avocado trees flanked the front door. These trees were old and towered above the house and the avocados grew to be as large as giant grapefruits.

There were two palm trees which the natives called coco trees, one at each end of the kidney shaped pool. I got to hate these trees as they spewed their seeds directly into the pool and I spent most of the summer dipping the brown pea sized seeds out of the pool. Behind the pool next to the sandstone wall was a papaya tree as well as a few banana trees.

Just outside the back kitchen door was a breadfruit tree and the rest of the garden to the right of the house was dotted with lemon and lime trees. Besides all the trees there were local flowers and greenery, too much for us to take care of without a local gardener who understood the care of these types of plants.

Chapter 9

August Record's Return to the United States

Four months later I received a package from Nate Adams containing the latest edition of *Reader's Digest* which had as its feature article *"The Latin Connection"* the story of August Ricord and the Paraguayan government corruption. Surprisingly, a month later, the Paraguayan Supreme Court ruled that the United States extradition request for August Ricord was valid, and his extradition could proceed. Within four days, all the formal documents had been signed and approved, stamped and certified, and registered in the judicial Registry of Paraguay.

After all this nit picking and back room politicking we finally were going to get Record out of here!

This was followed by a blur of cable traffic and telephone calls between our Ambassador and the State Department; US Customs Headquarters and the US Customs Agent on site; and my traffic with BNDD Headquarters and the Regional office in BA; and the Department of Justice in Washington, and the US Attorney's office in NYC, most of which contradicted and countermanded each other, with everyone in the US scrambling for press and TV coverage.

I can't really believe this, everyone is jockeying for fame and glory.

The US government finally decided, instead of using a military aircraft, it would charter a Pan Am Boeing 707 with a full flight crew on board to fly Ricord back to New York City where he would be formally arrested. There would be four US Customs and four BNDD agents on the flight, who would take charge of Ricord on the airplane for the nonstop flight back to NYC. All of the press briefings, interviews and photo ops on the Paraguayan end would be handled by the Ambassador and the Paraguayan Minister of Interior.

Meanwhile, I made plans for local security and the physical handover of Ricord from the Paraguayans to the US government.

After all the interagency problems of who was going to do what, when and where, this was a piece of cake for me.

After numerous meetings with my counterpart, Attorney General Campos Alum, it was finally decided that he, the Paraguayan government, will be responsible for Ricord's safety and security until he was handed over to me at plane side.

The day for the event arrived and the plan was for the plane, which had spent the night in Rio, to arrive in Asuncion at 9:00 AM, at which time the transfer of Ricord would take place, and we would be off to New York City. My thoughts were, *always remember to KISS it (keep it simple stupid) when possible.*

I had Carlos, my junior agent, drive me out to the airport, to arrive at 8:00 AM so I would have time for a cup of coffee and to make sure everything was going as planned. As we drove the ten kilometers from my house to the airport, I noticed soldiers stationed every two hundred meters along the highway to the airport.

Golly. This is the largest display of military power I have seen since I have been here.

At the airport the security was more impressive. There were soldiers at one hundred meter intervals around the entire airport facility and the entrance was blocked with two armored cars with machine guns that were locked and loaded.

Well, so much for an easy quiet departure.

After clearing the checkpoint we drove to the Director's office, where Major Lopez, dressed in his Air Force uniform, wearing a pistol belt and a .45 caliber automatic, was in deep conversation with two officers of the Guardia Naccional, who were also carrying side arms.

I got out of the car and walked over to the Major, smiled and said, "Hola, Major, nice day for an airplane ride."

"Senor Rayner, I am glad to see you. Are you going on the plane?'

"I sure am, Major. There aren't any problems, are there?"

"We were just discussing what we should do if there is an attempt to rescue Senor Ricord. Capitan Arnesa, here, thinks we should kill Ricord first and then kill the *traficantes*, but I don't think that is right. What do you think?"

"Well, Major, I think it is more likely that they will try to kill Ricord, so he can't tell the police about his associates and their plans."

"You're right, I didn't think of that. So what is the plan for today? They haven't told me many details, and I'm the director of the airport."

"I don't know much either. My job is to meet the plane as it pulls up, go out to talk to the Captain of the aircraft and when he gives me the O.K. I signal to the police and they bring Ricord, out to the plane and turn him over to me. They can drive him right out that gate by the VIP lounge. I am sure you will have a guard at the gate with the key. Simple, I hope."

"You are right, Senor Rayner, that was really the plan I had in mind. I'm glad you agree with it."

"Its fine Major; I will let you and the Capitan work out the details. Carlos and I are going to have a cup of coffee and a dulce. Please let me know when the tower has contact with the plane. And, of course, let me know when the Federales arrive with Senor Ricord."

As I was finishing my second blast of local caffeine doble, Jim Green, the US customs agent walked into the cafeteria and announced that the Major just told him the flight would be there in twenty minutes and the Federales would be there with Ricord in about a half hour. He and I briefly went over the plans and agreed on what should transpire.

Like clockwork, eighteen minutes later a beautiful blue Pan AM 707 touched down, rolled out, and taxied to the front of the terminal. By the time the engines were spooling down, a set of air steps was rolled out to the front door of the plane and the auxiliary power was plugged into the nose. As soon as the air steps were in place, I hurried up to the landing and was waiting when the steward popped the seal and opened the door.

I flashed him my badge and said, "I'm the Attaché with the US Embassy. Let me speak to the captain."

"Sure, come on up front."

In the cockpit, the flight crew was still going over their post flight check list. The steward introduced me to the captain, who asked, "What's with all these soldiers; there isn't going to be any trouble, is there?"

I told him, "Not likely, but the plan is to get loaded as quick as we can and get back in the air. Is there any reason you or your crew have to leave the aircraft?"

"Nope, we fueled up this morning in Rio and took on a complete food and beverage service for the flight back. So, we are good to go."

"That's great. As soon as our guest arrives, I'll bring him up the stairs and we can be off. Oh, could you tell those guys in the back this is a very delicate situation and the locals aren't all together happy. It would be better for them to stay on the plane. We don't want an international incident or anything to delay this thing."

The captain, with raised eyebrows, smiled and said, "A couple of those guys are real assholes. They were drinking a lot of booze yesterday on the flight down to Rio and then hit on the stewardess' last night. I'll keep them on board."

I hurried back down the steps and into the VIP lounge as Carlos was coming in the other door with the Major, who said, "They have just entered the gate and will be here in two minutes."

"That's good. Jim, when they pull up why don't you carry our bags out to the plane and stand at the top of the steps; when I take custody of Ricord, you can tell the pilot we are ready to roll, and he can start to wind up the engines so we can get out of here."

"Carlos, you stay here and make sure things go as we planned. Tell Campos Alum we don't want any ceremony at the aircraft and he can do all of the PR shit and be the hero of the day, or whatever, with the press and TV. If he needs any papers signed, you sign them in here, I don't want to fumble around for a ball point out there on the runway or have the damn papers blow away. Remember, keep your head down and if you catch any heat while I'm gone, just tell them I ordered you to do it."

"OK, Gordon, have a good flight."

I watched the convoy arrive; first, a military three quarter ton with a mounted .50 cal. gun, with ammunition belt in place and four NCOs with machine pistols in the back. This was followed by a Department of Interior Mercedes 700 series sedan, tinted windows and all, with a second three quarter ton equipped as the first one. This was followed by a military 6 by 6 with a squad of ten soldiers armed with rifles.

The convoy halted and I saw the limousine's right front door open and Campos Alum step out as eight NCOs jumped to the ground and faced outwards with their machine pistols at the ready and the squad from the 6 by 6 deployed facing out to the rear.

Then the rear doors of the limo opened, and two huge agents stepped out, guns in hand. *Man, they are taking this shit seriously.*

At last, one of the huge agents reached in the rear of the limo and dragged out a short, thin, bald headed man wearing jeans, a tee shirt and rimless wire glasses, like my grandfather wore. This was the notorious August Ricord, the Latin Connection, responsible for smuggling hundreds of kilos of heroin, the white death, into the United States.

Damn, why can't any of the big bad heavy hitters look like a gangster or a mobster, you know like Peter Lorrie, James Cagney, or Sidney Greenstreet, instead of looking like Casper Milqtoast?

I could see Carlos and Campos Alum talking and Carlos pointing to where I was standing by the air steps to the plane. Campos Alum nodded and returned to the Mercedes where he, Ricord and the two guards got in, and then the car came through the opened gate and pulled up beside me.

Campos Alum again got out of the car and, as we shook hands, said, "Well, Senor Rayner here is your prisoner. Take care of him."

Campos Alum gestured and the two guards pulled Ricord from the car. I was surprised to see Ricord was in handcuffs and asked the guard to take the cuffs off him, which he did. I looked at Ricord. He was sixty two years old, came up to about my chin and weighed about one hundred and ten pounds. I figured I could prevent him from doing anything, so I just motioned up the stairs and said, "After you, Senor."

Ricord nodded and headed up the stairs. I shook hands with Campos Alum and followed Ricord, catching up with him at the top of the steps. Putting my hand on his elbow I guided him into the aircraft as I signaled the steward to close it up and turned right into the cabin.

Immediately, we were surrounded by four agents, and before I could speak, one of them grabbed Ricord's wrist and slapped a handcuff on it, loudly announcing.

"US Customs, I hereby place you under arrest."

I responded, "I don't think so, he's in my custody."

"Who the fuck are you? Do you know who I am? I'm the US Customs ASAIC for New York and this is my collar and no one is going to screw me out of it! The Commissioner promised it would be mine."

"Well," I said, "Don't get your ass in an uproar. I don't care who you are or what your Commissioner promised you, but I don't work for you or him, so let's just cool down and talk about this. Oh, and by the way, since Mr. Ricord has been arrested at least once, I think the first thing to do would be to advise him of his rights under the Miranda Decision."

As the Customs ASAIC was turning bright red, another agent pushed his way through our little crowd, stuck out his and hand and said, "I'm Jerry Costas, BNDD Group Two Supervisor in New York City. You must be Rayner."

"That's me. What's all the fuss with this Customs asshole?"

"Ha, that's funny. If you think this is bad, wait till you see what happens when we get to New York. When I called this morning, they told me they are going to have a big press conference, with all the TV and newspaper people at Kennedy when we arrive. Mr. Ingersoll (BNDD Administrator), the Commissioner of Customs, the US Attorney for the Southern District, a Deputy Attorney General from main Justice, the Chief of Police for NYC, the colonel from the New

York State Police and probably someone from New Jersey will all be there, all trying to get in front of the cameras."

"Well, shit. You all do whatever you have to do. All I want is a stiff drink and something to eat. Do you think you can get the stewardess to bring me something? With this whole airplane to ourselves, I think I can find a seat and besides, the pilot is about to start his takeoff roll out.

Chapter 10

Blond Blue Eyed Lady

One Saturday, while the family was enjoying a slow, free morning at home just reading and lulling about, there was a knock at the front door. Greg and Jo jumped from their chairs and ran to see who was there because un-expected visitors were not usual in Paraguay. Visits were usually arranged in order that the host could be prepared for the visitor.

At the door stood a young man who was about thirty years old, dressed in military fatigues with his hat in hand. He had a ready smile and with military crispness went on to tell us what he wanted.

"Ma'am, I am Captain Anderson and I am attached to the U.S. MIL Group here in Paraguay. I will be shipping out to my new post in a few weeks, my wife and children will be going with me and we need to find a new home for our dog, Damita. She has been part of our family for two years and gets along well with my three children. The family sent me out today to find her a good home."

Of course Greg and Jo, who have always had a pet in the home, were all smiles and turned to me and said, "We can take her, can't we? Pleaaasee."

The young man went on to say, "She had been part of another family before we got her and she has been trained to alert us if someone, especially a Paraguayan, comes unto the property. Also she would be very lonely without children around."

I have always had a soft spot in my heart for animals so it did not take too long for me to say yes to this very charming and caring officer at my door. During the next few days as I was talking to my friends, I learned that the custom among the foreigners living in Asuncion was to pass a well trained dog from one family to another.

At the end of the week, the young officer returned with Damita (Little Lady). She followed the young man into the house and on seeing the children; she stretched out her two paws on the floor in front of her and looked longingly at them as she wagged her tail slowly back and forth.

The three children were now on the floor, slowly putting out their hands to pet her and talking to her, "Damita, come here. My, aren't you a pretty dog. You do want to stay with us, don't you?"

She had long blond hair, blue eyes and appeared to be smiling. She was an instant hit and our home and hearts were hers.

In the following weeks, we learned her worth. We had forgotten to close the gate to the drive way and a bearded, unkempt beggar had made his way three quarters of the distance up the drive to the back door. Damita alerted on him. She did not attack but kept on barking as she backed him down the driveway and out to the gate. We also found out why she would become very alert and bark when Paraguayans walked by. It was apparent they did not like dogs because when a Paraguayan man or boy passed by the property they would throw sticks or stones at her or slap a stick on the gate as they passed by.

She was an integral part of our family life for the two and a half years we lived in Paraguay. During that time she had a litter of nine puppies. They were all different colors but only one was blond in color, but no blue eyes. Before we left Paraguay, we also made sure she had a good home.

Chapter 11

Trip to Buenos Aires

Shopping on Avenida Florida

One of the few times I was able to travel out of Paraguay with Gordon he asked me to go with him to Buenos Aires for a regional meeting.

In surprise, I said, "How long will we be staying and what will we be doing? I really don't have anything to wear."

"Don't worry. We will just be gone for a few days and there are no big events scheduled. Besides you can go shopping when you get there."

"Wow, this is going to be a holiday. I'm getting out of Dodge and I can go shopping in a store instead of in a catalogue. When are we leaving?"

I had not been to Buenos Aires before and I was bubbling with anticipation. When we got on the plane, we were surprised to see that George Belk and John Enright, two of Gordon's superiors, were also on the plane and were sitting across the aisle from us. The agents were soon talking shop and I was by the window taking in the scenery.

The sun was shining when we left Asuncion and there wasn't a cloud in the sky and I could see the winding rivers and the green forests of the area. This flight from Asuncion to Buenos Aires had a stop in Resistencia, Argentina. As we flew toward Resistencia, the clouds began to form and there was a thick cloud cover by the time we neared the airport. When we broke out of the clouds, we were not lined up with the runway. Although the pilot had followed the VOR homing beacon on the way in, we were to the right of the runway.

The calm pilot's voice came over the speaker. "We will be going around again to make this landing."

Up until now most of the passengers had been waiting calmly for the bump of the tires on the landing strip and the sound of the reverse thrusters. Now everyone was on alert and all eyes were intent on the clouds and the land below us. The cloud cover was at about one thousand feet which didn't leave much air space below us.

Everyone was thinking we would have to return to the clouds to make another landing approach. However, this pilot had another idea in mind. Instead of going into the clouds he banked sharply and made a three hundred and sixty degree turn to the left but stayed under the clouds. He apparently was not about to lose sight of the runway. The plane had an approximate wing span of one hundred and fifty feet so those of us who were on the left side of the plane felt we were very close to the ground. In fact I could almost distinguish the facial features of a man on a tractor and actually saw a man sitting in a car reading his newspaper.

When I looked around to see how the passengers were reacting to this maneuver, I noticed all of them were very quiet and had a white knuckle grip on their seats. That's when I became aware that George Belk, who usually had an in control demeanor about him, appeared to be very nonchalant about the whole affair as he read his newspaper. However, I did notice the paper he was reading was upside down.

The pilot circled around and set the plane down smoothly on the tarmac. When he came to a halt everyone rose and gave him a standing ovation.

Passengers deplaned and others boarded and we continued our flight to Buenos Aries through the clouds. We all had an hour and a half to calm down. Then we would be ready to see the bright lights of Buenos Aries also known as the Paris of the South.

It was a bright sunny spring afternoon in October of 1972, when we landed in Buenos Aires and I was quickly up into the aisle full of anticipation to take in the sights of this renowned city of South America.

We took a cab to the Sheraton Hotel and after settling in for a few days stay, we took a walk to look for a place to eat.

As we left the hotel, Gordon guided me to the right saying, "You have to see Nuevo de Julio (9th of July). It is the biggest avenue you will ever see."

He was right. There were twelve lanes of traffic, six going north and six going south and there were parks scattered between some of the lanes. It was spring time, and the trees were varied shades of green, and the flowers were abloom in all their glory. It looked very serene and lovely as the sun was beginning to fade slowly in the west. The only thing to spoil the mood was the noise of the cars zooming by on all twelve lanes. With that beautiful view etched in our minds, we found a small café for a relaxing evening meal.

Gordon explained that he had to be at the embassy for a meeting about eight o'clock in the morning and I could sleep in and walk to the embassy which was about five or six blocks away.

He went on to say, "The easiest way to go would be up Avenida Florida which is the most famous shopping area in Buenos Aries and perhaps all of South America. It will probably cost me, but you will enjoy the shops."

The next morning I got up late, had a few sweet rolls and the usual Latin café con leche, and prepared for my shopping trip on Avenida Florida. I found it easily as it was only a block from the hotel. However, I was very surprised to run into a strong military presence. On every other block there were two federal police armed with submarine guns and another with an attack dog.

As I turned the corner onto Avenida Florida, I saw the elaborate signs and logos of the many shops that beckoned to me. I literally caught my breath on seeing this array of goods. My last year of shopping had been confined to a catalogue and the primitive shops of Asuncion. I just stood for a moment to drink in all the sights, sounds, and smell of real honest to goodness shops. They stretched as far as I could see and I had the whole morning to browse and buy, if I wanted. Gordon had told me the money exchange rate was also in our favor as the American dollar was worth on hundred and twenty five pesos. That put many extra pesos in my pocket.

There were several leather shops, a Sterns jewelry store, several cosmetic shops of global renown, as well as perfume shops. The wine shops were deep and lined with gold labeled bottles. The gold and silver shops had huge displays of gold jewelry, frames and home decorations as well as many silver services for twelve arranged in ornate wooden chests. Woolen shops and clothing stores were also part of the mix.

As I walked along I noticed there were several kinds of leather shops. One shop specialized in hand bags and belts, another had leather clothing. There was a shop for equestrian gear, one for luggage, as well as one for shoes and boots. Anything the upscale shopper would wish to buy was available.

I came to realize each international cosmetic firm had a store of their own as did the perfume shops. The gold and silver stores also featured rings, bracelets, vintage tea services and big silver serving trays. What seemed unusual to me were the displays of silver spurs, which I finally realized were for the gauchos and especially the tourists.

After about ten minutes of ingesting this feast for the eyes, I finally ventured into a store. It was early spring and still a bit cool, so my first impulse was to buy a warm sweater. So into a wool shop I went and found a multi colored pullover that I felt would go with anything. I tried on the sweater, and it felt so nice and warm I decided to buy it and wear it out of the store. As I paid for it, my old blouse went into a bag.

I continued my stroll and came upon a leather shop that sold clothes, and they had a beautiful black leather skirt displayed in the window. *Oh, it would go well with my sweater."* Into the store I went. I tried on the skirt as well as a leather vest. They looked great, fit well, and I again decided to wear them out of the store. The purchase was paid for and the old clothes went into the bag. I was on a roll.

As I neared the end of Avenida Florida, I came upon a shoe and boot store that had black soft leather boots on display.

Now they would go well with my new outfit. Oh, they are a bit pricey but are within my budget due to the good exchange rate. What the heck. I've come this far. I may as well go all the way."

Again the new purchase was worn out of the store, and the old shoes went into the bag. As I walked along I had a thought. Which is the real me? The one walking down the street in this spiffy new outfit or am I in the bag?

Another block of window shopping, and I arrived at the American Embassy. On entering, the Marine guard on duty asked for my identification, then told me how to get to the DEA offices. The secretary told me Gordon was in a meeting and would be out shortly and I could wait for him in the next room. As we chatted she received a call that Gordon was in a room down the hall and to meet him there.

I found the room, opened the door and threw in the bag and sashayed in behind it and asked, "How do you like the new me?"

He chuckled and with a leering look said, "You look great! Can I take you to lunch?"

Chapter 12

Working with Informants

Working informants in Paraguay was extremely difficult as the city had only a population of 300,000. Much like a small town, the majority of the people was related or knew each other in some fashion.

My first informant was the Money Changer. As in most South American countries there was an official government rate of exchange and there was the 'real' exchange rate which was much higher in favor of cashing US dollars. It may have been illegal, but the money changers plied their trade openly in the commercial section of Asuncion without police interference. In fact, I met the Money Changer shortly after I had arrived, when he made his usual visit to the US Embassy to exchange funds for the American employees. He would even accept personal checks drawn on a US bank for exchange to Guaranies, the local currency.

I was sitting in my office on the second floor of the Embassy, where only US citizens were allowed, when the US Marine Guard called. He told me there was someone at Post #1, the front door to the Embassy, who insisted that he meet with me. I went downstairs and was met by the Money Changer. He was about 40 years old, five foot two inches tall, of slender build, wearing a suit jacket and carrying a brief case full of money, Paraguayan, US, Brazilian, Argentine and Bolivian. He said it is very important we talk but not in public.

After the US Marine Guard checked his briefcase, the Money Changer and I went up to the BNND office. With great curiosity, I showed him into my office and told Donnie, my secretary, to get us a couple of sodas from the cafeteria.

When she left to get the sodas, the Money Changer introduced himself and said, "I know who you are and what your job is besides just trying to get August Ricord extradited. There are many contrabandista pilots here in Asuncion who smuggle electronics, wrist watches, Levis and liquor from Panama. Rather than fly back to Panama empty, they are able to smuggle drogas back to Panama and you are here to stop them."

Jesus, this guy is reading from the BNDD Operational Briefing Book.

"How do you know that?"

He laughed, "I may be a simple peon, but I am very much up on international news, as that affects my business with the various rates of exchange."

"You are certainly right about what our job is, but how can you help me?"

He said, "Señor Rayner, I and my associates do business all over the city and I have runners who hang around the high class hotels, restaurants, casinos and bars where the foreigners go to drink and find women. When the runner sees a foreigner flashing a large amount of money and spending it freely, they make an approach on them to see if they need help in exchanging some of their money at a rate above what they could get at a local hotel or bank. If the foreigner is agreeable, the runner calls me and I come and do the exchange. In fact, I have done business several times with some of these foreigners and they have come to trust me and look me up when they are in town."

"Aren't you afraid of a rip off?"

He laughed, "There is very little crime against people here in Paraguay and besides I bring a body guard with me to make sure there isn't any funny business."

"Who is your body guard?"

"Oh, he is an old friend, and is a private investigator, so he carries a gun. Maybe you should meet him too. He might be able to provide you with information."

I then fingerprinted, photographed and filled out a personal history form on the Money Changer and he became Informant S-1.

Two days later, the Fat Man, the Money Changer's body guard, showed up at the Embassy to be signed up as Informant S-2. The Fat Man was about forty years old, five feet eight inches tall, two hundred and fifty pounds, with a round face and a full head of curly black hair, casually dressed and well-spoken. He declared, I am one of the few licensed private investigators in Paraguay and have connections with the National Police and many government employees, as well as the commercial smugglers and the underworld."

I asked, "What kind of underworld is there in Paraguay? This is almost a police state and I didn't think there was any crime. The police even watch my house."

He shrugged and said, "Oh, you know, people that are into providing American cigarettes, liquor, wrist watches and electronics to the local market. Since all luxuries have such high import taxes, they will smuggle and sell anything to make a profit. And, since they have the apparatus set up, they can just as easily smuggle other things out of the country. I can provide you with information on their identities, their aircraft numbers and any plans they may be making to carry drugs north."

"Do you think you can do this? Drug smuggling is usually a very secret business."

"Señor Rayner," he continued, "Here in Paraguay, there are very few real secrets. The police are either bribed or just look the other way at these things. They are afraid that they may be interfering with some big official's business and if they report it they may be sent to an undesirable post out in the campo, lose their job or get killed."

"Do the police know what you are doing?"

"Si señor, not everyone is corrupt. Most people are opposed to this and want to do something to stop it. The top sergeant of the Federal Police is a friend of mine and knows what I am doing."

To say the least, this was all very unusual and I knew I would not be doing much undercover work in Paraguay.

Several months later on a Friday afternoon the Money Changer arrived in my office, out of breath and very excited. "Señor Rayner, I have information! A contrabandista is flying out this afternoon in his plane and is headed for Panama with drogas The guy was at a bar last night, throwing around a lot of money and bragging how he was going to have a lot more when he got back.."

"Okay! This is great! What kind of plane is it and what is the tail number?"

"It's a Loadstar. The tail number is N499, I think. And his name is Juan Cierva."

"I'll send a cable to Panama. Come back on Monday and I'll tell you what happens."

The Money Changer left and I sent an immediate cable to the Panama Office laying out the details of the information. I spent an anxious weekend. This was the first actionable information I had gathered in Paraguay.

On Monday, I couldn't wait and had pestered the Comm office every hour to see if a message had arrived. At about 3:00 PM a Comm officer walked into my office with a message in his hand. "Are you looking for this?" he smirked.

I snatched the message from his hand and read the following:

Subject A/C arrived 1 AM Saturday. Panama National Police (PNP) and BNDD agents searched A/C. Negative results. Pilot, Juan Cierva, still being interrogated by PNP. Extensive search of A/C for hidden compartments by PNP is continuing.

Wm. Plase, SAIC

About three months later at a Regional conference, Bill Plase and I, along with the other SAICs, were sharing a happy hour at the Regional Director's house when the discussion turned to how we could better deter smugglers from using A/C to fly drugs north. Bill sputtered in his drink and laughed hilariously, "Hell, you could do like Rayner did. Just call Panama."

George, the SAIC from Brazil, asked, "What do you mean Bill?"

Bill then related the information I had sent and how the PNP had reacted. He said, "The pilot of this Loadstar got real smart ass with the police and they took offense when he said that they couldn't find their ass with both hands, much less find any drugs on his plane. The officer in charge who spoke English grabbed Cierva, threw him on his knees, pulled out his .45, stuck it to the back of Cierva's head, cocked the hammer and told him he was about to die. You should have seen Cierva. He pissed his pants and started crying. He gave up everything he had ever done, who he had done it with and even told them his real name. He pleaded that he would confess to anything they wanted him to, only don't kill him. "

All of us rolled on the ground laughing hysterically.

Bill continued, "Hell, when I left to come down here yesterday, Cierva's plane had the wings off and parts of the fuselage lying on the ground. That thing will never fly again and Cierva is out of the smuggling business for good if he ever gets out of jail. Maybe we should do that more often."

Chapter 13

Safari, Paraguay Style

After we had been in Paraguay for about two months, things began to settle down. We had moved into our house, had our furniture delivered and in place, the kids were in school and our car had arrived. I had hired a secretary and the office was up and running. One Friday at Happy Hour I was drinking at the Marine House, when Art Kohl asked me if I wanted to go hunting in the Chaco, I instantly accepted.

Open mouth, quickly insert foot!

Art, who was a former Marine Guard at the Embassy, had fallen in love with a local girl and had gotten married. When his enlistment in the Corps was over he returned to Asuncion. Though his father in law was from a well to do family by Paraguayan standards, he could not find a place in his business for his gringo son in law. This resulted in Art getting the job of managing the commissary at the Embassy. His connections with the Paraguayan community were a great asset when it came to getting the shipping containers of commissary provisions from the States. Customs procedures were very tedious and there was much pilfering, regardless of how much *mordida* was paid.

On the humorous side, we received one container from which they had pilfered two cases of Jack Daniels whiskey, and, oddly also a case of liter bottles of Log Cabin Maple Syrup. Two weeks later I was in an 'international' liquor store in downtown Asuncion and there on the shelf beside our hijacked Jack Daniels I spied bottles of Log Cabin Maple Syrup. I told Art about the syrup, and surprisingly a week later it appeared on the shelf at the commissary. I never asked how it got there.

Now back to our trip, Art explained that since the following Friday was a holiday, we could leave early on Thursday and drive about 200 kilometers into the Chaco to one of the ranch houses that his in laws owned. There we could hunt deer and anything else we wanted to including the local wild pigs, much like our javelinas. Then we could return to Asuncion on Sunday.

"Ah, Art, you drive an old Toyota pickup and I have a brand new 4 door Ford LTD which my wife wouldn't think of letting me drive up there on those dirt roads. Where are we going to get the wheels for this expedition?"

"Well, Gordon, Jim from communications and I were talking about that and he explained that he is only an 'enlisted man' and can't requisition a vehicle; However, you are a chief of section on the Embassy staff and can get one from the motor pool with no problem."

"Gee, Art, I'll have to think about it. I'll ask the Admin Officer on Monday."

"Already got that covered, he said it wouldn't be a problem. All you have to do is sign for it and you got it."

"Art, if you're setting me up, I'll cut your balls off and feed them to you."

"Man, you know I wouldn't do anything like that, we're friends."

"Okay, Art, who else is going with us?"

"Well, it's only Jim and me and you so far. Why don't you bring Jack, your partner, with us? The more the merrier."

"That might not be a bad idea. He seems stressed out. Maybe a little hunting trip is just what he needs. And, hey, we have the room, why don't I ask my son, Greg. He would eat that shit up and it would give us a chance for some father and son bonding."

"Then we're on. I'll handle the logistics. I'll get the drinks, beer, soda, and the water plus the ice and cooler chests. Ah, also some food, coffee and other stuff. Once you get the okay on Monday I'll get with the Colonel and make sure we get a good carryall as well as an extra spare tire, auxiliary gas can and other stuff for the trip."

"Hey, didn't you tell me this ranch was right off the main highway. What do we need all the extra stuff for?"

"Well, we might want to do some minor off-roading, you know. You can't be over prepared. There ain't no AAA out there."

"Art, this is getting bigger and bigger as we go on. What kind of sleeping arrangements do they have?"

"Not to worry, they have hammocks on a screened in veranda and the caretaker's wife will cook for us. The big thing we have to worry about is how much ice we can carry with us. Otherwise, we'll be drinking warm bourbon and warm beer."

Just about then, Jack walked in, grabbed a drink at the bar and walked over to us and said, "Well, Art, did you talk him into it?"

"You bastards! This is just one big set up. The only reason you asked me was to get the carryall! But it does sound like fun so I'll go along with your crazy scheme. Let me out of here, I'm going to the house and tell my son. I can't wait to see his reaction."

When I got to the house, I pulled up in the driveway, blew the horn and waited for one of the kids or Vicky to come open the gate. First out of the house was our blonde dog, Damita, barking her fool head off as usual.

"Good dog!" I cried, "Keep all them bad guys off the property."

Then my son came out and opened the gate. "You're home early, Dad, what's up? They throw you out of the Marine House?"

"Just what I need. A smart ass comedian for a son. No, Ace, I came home to see you. I need to talk to you."

"Oh, honest Dad, it wasn't me. Jo must have done it. And anyway, I'm sorry if I did do it and I won't do it again. I promise."

"It's nothing like that. Come on in the house, I have a surprise and I want the whole family to hear it the first time, so I don't have to repeat it a million times. Have Vicky get me one of those Wallbangers while I change clothes and then I'll tell you my surprise."

Five minutes later I walked back into the living room and announced to the whole family that the guys and I were going on a hunting trip to the Chaco next weekend and I thought Greg might want to come along.

"You mean like a safari!! Do I get to take a gun? Are we going to shoot wild animals? Who is going with us? Where are we going?"

"Whoa, Son. We're going with Art Kuhl up to his father-in-law's ranch; it's about 200 klicks up the Chaco Highway. Jim, the communication Officer, and Jack are going with us. I'll talk to the principal about you missing school on Thursday, and with Friday being a holiday; you'll only miss one day of school. We'll be coming back Sunday, so it shouldn't be any sweat."

Ella Mae smiled, "That sounds like fun. You two haven't had much of a chance to do things together since we've been here. Vicki, you can come in, I know you've been listening and even though you don't understand English, what do you think of the idea?"

Vicki entered, carrying my Wallbanger, "Yo no se, senora, but it sounds good to me."

All three of the kids chimed in, "Vicki, you don't speak English! Remember?" and we all burst out laughing, even Vicki.

The following Wednesday evening, I laid out all my guns, equipment, boots and camouflage clothes for the trip. There was my AR-15, my .303 Enfield, my new 12 gauge Remington pump shotgun, my old double sweet sixteen, my 9mm S&W with 2 extra magazines and my .38 snub nose. I also had my Marine Corps K-Bar fighting knife, my hide-a-way stiletto, my cartridge belt, ammo packs, first aid pack, compass, canteens and shoulder harness.

Wait a minute, Gordon; you are just going hunting with your son and some guys for two days. We are not going to assault a fortified position or have to call in air support and artillery.

Well, after this reality check I decided on a pair of Levis, long sleeve shirt, and my lace up hunting boots. We would take a shotgun each, the sweet sixteen for my son, and the new Remington pump for me. And of course, my 9mm as a sidearm, you know, just in case. Our tooth brushes, a wash cloth, and a clean pair of underwear for each of us as well as a roll of US toilet paper went into a small overnight bag. We were ready for the big day.

Ella Mae drove us over to the Embassy and dropped us off in the rear parking lot of the Embassy where the carryall was parked. We were the first ones there, so after we loaded our gear in the vehicle, Greg and I went up the back stairs of the Embassy to my office. I had to make sure the world wasn't going to go to hell in a hand basket while I was away. As usual, Donnie, my secretary, had everything under control and only needed my signature on a couple of reports.

"Come on, Son; let's see if the other guys are here yet."

As we came down the back steps, I could hear loud laughter coming from the office by the back door, where all the Embassy drivers hung out. Even the retired Paraguayan Colonel in charge was laughing so hard he had tears coming down his cheeks. I walked up to the Colonel and asked, "What's the big joke? You guys are always so formal."

The Colonel just shook his head and pointed out to our carryall.

Oh crap! There was Jack, dressed just like 'Paladin' from the old TV Western series. Black cowboy hat with a silver concho band, black cowboy shirt with pearl snaps on the pockets, black pants tucked into fourteen inch tooled black cowboy boots with two inch heels and a broad black belt with silver conchos adorning it, secured with a massive silver belt buckle.

As Greg and I walked towards the vehicle, Greg said, "Gees, dad is he for real?"

"I told you it was going to be a fun trip, son. Just don't laugh at him."

As I got closer, I could see Jack struggling to put some kind of holster or sheath onto his belt. "Hey, Jack, what's the problem?"

"Oh, I can't get this damn scabbard for my Bowie knife to fit on my belt."

"I see. That looks like an awfully big scabbard for a Bowie knife; it looks like it's made for a sword or something."

"Well, right after I got to Asuncion, I figured I might need a Bowie knife, so I went down to this auto body shop to see if they could make me one."

"Jack, an auto body shop? Why the hell would you go there for a frigging Bowie knife?"

"You don't know shit about fighting knives, do you?"

"Well, not really. All I have is my K-Bar and I left that at the house today."

"Ha, these gunfighter magazines all say the best steel for a killing knife is a leaf spring from a VW Beetle. So I found me a shop and had them make me one. You know, heat the steel, beat it on an anvil, plunge it in water, and do this over and over again. Shaping it and hammering it until it became case hardened. Here! Look at this beauty."

"Easy, Jack, that thing looks evil. How long is it?"

"You know a Bowie knife, or as we call them, an Arkansas tooth pick, usually has a blade up to fourteen or sixteen inches long. So I thought I might as well get a real BIG one. This sucker has a twenty-two inch blade and genuine Lapacho wood grips. It cost me a pretty penny, but it's worth it. Then I found this leather shop and had them make a sheath for it, but I don't think it'll fit my belt."

"Let me see it, Jack. Wow, this sucker is heavy, but it does have some good balance to it."

"Yeah, you need it balanced, if you're going to throw it at somebody and it has to be heavy so it won't break when it hits a rib or something when you gut the son of a bitch. There I have the scabbard on the belt. Let me have the blade so I can be sure it carries well. See, how does it look?"

"It looks fine, Jack, just put it away until we get out in the monte; you're not going to need it here at the Embassy. Besides, it does look a little out of place, don't you think?"

"Fuck 'em! These guys need to see what a real gunfighter looks like."

"Jack, we aren't going to a gunfight. We're only going to go hunting for a few days. You know shoot a few animals, drink a few beers, and have a few laughs."

"Okay, I guess you're right, but watch this!" Swish!!!!!!! He raised his right hand above his head and swept the blade down to the left across his body.

"Christ, Jack, put that thing away before someone gets hurt! I'm serious man; cool down; take that fugging sword off and be cool!"

"All right, I guess I did get carried away a bit."

"Greg, you stay here with Jack and get the gear stowed, I'm going to find out where Art and Jim are. They should have been here by now... Oh, speak of the devil, here they come and it looks like they have all the provisions and stuff with them. Maybe we can get on the road on time for once."

After all the gear was stowed, the gas cans filled, and the two extra spare tires were checked, we finally left the compound. Art drove as we proceeded west on Avenida Lopez on our great adventure. Jack was in the front passenger seat and Jim, Greg and I sat in the back. We proceeded out the paved road past the International airport and shortly came to the ferry at Villa Hayes where we said goodbye to the paved roads. Once across the river we would be in the Chaco with only a dirt road that stretched all the way to Bolivia, some 500 kilometers out through the primitive arid landscape.

Fortunately, there wasn't much traffic waiting for the ferry, so we had just enough time to grab a cold six pack of St. Pauli Girl from the super tienda before boarding for the ten minute trip across the Rio Paraguaya. Once we were on the other side, the traffic of buses and 18 wheeler freight trucks rapidly thinned out, to the point that we could drive with the windows down without eating a bunch of dust. It really wasn't a bad road, and we were making about 30-40 klicks/hour throughout the afternoon.

As the sun slowly settled in the clear western sky, I started to relax and think maybe it wasn't going to be such a disaster after all. About five o'clock, we stopped for a bladder break, I asked Art, "What are the plans for dinner? You said we have about four more hours to go."

"I am the man with the plan", bragged Art. "We are about twenty klicks from Pozo Colorado, (Red Springs), a small town with a gas station, tienda and most importantly the best restaurant in the Chaco, recommended by Drunkin Swine. I figure we'll have dinner there and push on to the ranch. We should get there by midnight."

That sounds great! This is a pretty rough area and I haven't seen a ranch house for *the last fifteen minutes.*

"Art, are we going to have to play cowboys and Indians in this cantina?"

"Oh, yeah, I forgot to mention it. We probably should all wear our guns from here on out. Not that there is going to be any problems, but we want these people to know we ain't no tourists and not to screw with us."

"I didn't see that mentioned in the tourist guide book. I'm glad you told us."

Just after dark, we arrived at the cantina/bar/restaurant/gas station/tienda and pulled into the parking area, which surprisingly had fifteen freight trucks and pickups in the lot. Art mentioned that the reason for the town's existence was it had the only sweet water springs within an area of fifty miles. There was plenty of other ground water available, but it had the strong odor of sulfur, which made it hard to drink unless you were very desperate.

As we got out of the carryall, I told Greg, "If any shit goes down, just watch me and stay close, we'll try to make it back to the truck. Otherwise stay low and be cool."

The five of us walked up to the doors, opened them and eased slowly through them, trying to give our eyes time to adjust to the dimly lit interior. Well, just as in the old western movies, the conversation stopped, and all the patrons turned to look at us. I immediately noticed that though most of the diners were carrying side arms, no one had a fast draw rig or shoulder holster and did not appear threatening.

The manager quickly came up and with big fawning smile greeted us, "We have a nice table over on the side if you want dinner or you could all go to the bar."

Art said, "No problema, just a table for dinner off to one side of the room."

"Si, senor, this way."

To a bystander, it would seem funny to watch all of us trying to grab the seats so we could sit with our backs to the wall. Force of habit I guess. Our anxieties proved to be unfounded, as the clients were simply ranchers and farmers from the surrounding area and this was the place to go for an evening out. The next closest town was the Mennonite farming community of Filadelfia, 100 klicks to the north.

We all ordered a plate of stew that contained pieces of unknown meat, potatoes, mandioca and carrots, with the local corn bread on the side and bottles of St. Pauli Girl, even for my son, as I did not know what the local water might do to our gringo stomachs.

Forty five minutes later we had fueled the carryall and were back on the road, with only our headlights to complement the multitude of stars piercing the ebon darkness. There could have been mountains or canyons just off either side of the road and we would not have seen them in the pitch darkness.

Thank God, Art was driving. There was total blackness except for the headlights. Not knowing where we were going, the rest of us would have been completely lost. About midnight, we slowed down and turned off onto a dirt track to the right of the road. We drove about two more klicks, the trees and brush scraping the sides of the vehicle.

Man, if this isn't the right road, how are we even going to turn around, much less get out of here?

We came to a small clearing in the road, and Art announced, "Well, we're here."

"Where is here? I don't see a damn thing."

"Man, Gordon, you really have lost your night vision. There, off to left at ten o'clock, see the kerosene lamp? The manager must have gotten the message we were coming and left the light on for us."

"I see it now, is that where we're going to sleep?"

"The lamp is probably at the ranch house. We'll drive up and check. The bunk house is about fifty yards beyond it. We'll have to use the headlights to help us get the stuff unloaded and set up the hammocks. I think everything else can wait until morning."

"I'll check with the manager and make sure he knows we aren't some fucking banditos, and come shoot our asses off."

"You guys hang here; I'll be back in a minute. And, don't wander away. We ain't going to go looking for you if you get lost. And, that does mean you, Jack."

Art returned shortly with Sr. Pena, the ranch manager, who showed us over to the bunk house, with its wide screened veranda, and six hammocks slung along the perimeter. He showed us the outhouse about ten yards out the back.

His parting comment was, "If you have to use it during the night, be sure to wear shoes, we don't have any snakes here, but there are spiders, scorpions and centipedes that bite like hell. Be careful. There will be coffee in the morning."

Before Mr. Pena left to go back to the main house, we fired up the Coleman lantern and made quick work of getting ready for bed, hanging our shirts and jeans on nails in the wall and placing our shoes close by the hammocks.

As I handed my flashlight to Greg, I said, "Good night Ace. When you put your shoes back on in the morning, shake them out first, the scorpions and spiders like to hide in dark places. It can be quite a surprise to find one in your shoe."

Jack, who I had learned had no camping experience at all, said, "That's just one of your bullshit stories, you ain't scaring me."

"Whatever, but put your gun in the holster and hang it on the wall, instead of keeping it in your hammock, you might grab it and blow your dick off in the dark."

Everyone else laughed. We each got a cold beer; except Greg, who had a Coke. Art turned off the lantern and we all lay there in the dark, sipping the cold beer, taking the last long drag on a Marlboro and listening to the night noises closing in around us. We all were soon dead to the world.

The next thing I knew, it was daylight, the screen door slammed and I lay there with my eyes closed, smelling the delicious aroma of the brewing coffee, lit up the best Marlboro of the day and started to mull over our safari plans in my mind.

I talked to Art and suggest that while we were hunting, we would keep Jack close to either Jim or him on a flank, so Jack had only one direction to shoot, as opposed to his being in the middle of the skirmish line and being able to shoot to both sides. This would lower the risk by half, that Jack might shoot one of us. Also, I would keep Greg with me on the other flank of the line to lower his chances of shooting anyone but me.

Over our first cup of coffee, I again mentioned this plan to Art. He thought I was being over cautious, but by the time breakfast was over, he had reconsidered my suggestion and agreed with me. "How the hell do you think of things like this?"

"It's the seven P plan, Art. Proper Prior Planning Prevents Piss Poor Performance. I try to use it all the time."

"That is really neat; I'll try to remember it. All right, I talked to the foreman and he said that the best chance to find some deer is going to be by the stock tank about two klicks east of here. It's one of the few watering holes close by. So, let's finish up and we'll drive out and see where it is."

Ten minutes later we were on our way. The whole landscape reminded me of the country around Laredo, Texas, mostly flat, dry, dusty sand and dirt. There was little grass, lots of cactus and scrubby mesquite trees no more than ten to twelve feet tall. What the ranchers would call hard scrabble cattle country, maybe able to support one steer for every ten acres.

We drove up the trail until we could see the top of the windmill at the tank, Art pulled the truck to a stop, and we quietly got out of the vehicle and started to unload our shotguns from the rear. I carried my 12 gauge pump up to the right rear passenger side door, uncased it and started explaining the gun to my son, who reached in the rear seat and got out the box of shells.

"Let me do it, Dad, I know how."

"Alright, Ace, here, it's all yours."

Bang!!!

I felt a splatter of mud against the back of my right leg and saw the mud puddle in the ditch next to me exploding. *Son of a Bitch!!!*

I pushed my son into the open door, and wheeled around, pulling my 9 mm S&W out of the holster, and throwing the safety off. Some bastard was trying to kill me!

There was Jack, his shotgun still smoking in his hands.

"You idiot! What the hell are you trying to do! You just missed blowing my fucking leg off."

"Wait, Gordon, don't shoot! Put down the gun! I was only checking the shot pattern of my shotgun. It was an accident. "

"Jack, you dummy, if I so much as see you come close to pointing that gun towards anybody, I'm going to shove it up where the sun don't shine."

"Son, are you all right?"

"Yeah, pop, you didn't have to throw me all the way in the truck. He was shooting at you, not me."

Well, that broke all of us up into laughter - a great way to calm down what had become a very tense situation.

Art said, "Well, we might as well relax for a while, that damn shot spooked anything there was around here. Let me check the map and see where else we can go."

While Art, Jim and I lit up Marlboros and started trying to decipher Art's hand drawn map, Jack had put on his Bowie Knife rig, walked over to a large Lapacho tree and drew out his big blade. We just stared at him and I unsnapped my holster. *What is he going to do now?*

Jack took about ten paces from the tree, whirled and threw his weapon at it. It missed! The three of us started to laugh, "What the hell are you doing?"

Jack retrieved his blade, turned to us and said, "Well, that accident with the shotgun upset me and I want to calm my nerves by throwing my knife. It should settle me down."

"Well, just don't hurt yourself. And son, don't get in his way."

We studied the map for about five minutes, finally decided which way was which and where we wanted to go. Then I heard Greg say, "Jack, if you can't get the knife to stick, maybe you aren't throwing it hard enough. It is just bouncing off the tree."

"Yeah, maybe you're right. Ugh!" I turned just as Jack threw the knife with all his might at the tree.

Boing! The knife hit the tree dead center, but not on the point. Instead it hit flat on its side and shattered into two pieces. Well, so much for case hardened VW spring Bowie knives.

After that, the rest of the day was anticlimactic. When we got close to a water tank, two of us would quietly circle the tank about 100 yards off to a side and the other three of us spread out in a skirmish line and started to sweep towards the tank. We hoped the game in the area would be driven towards the waiting pair of hunters. We kept this up for several hours, going from one tank to the next, getting always further away from the ranch house and deeper into the monte. If we were hunting for food for supper it would have been a hungry night.

Finally, hot, tired and thirsty, we decided to call it quits and head back to the ranch. Standing by the carryall, slowly sipping our first cold beers of the day, I looked at Art and said, "Well, which way do we go, Tonto?"

"Screw you, Rayner, the best I can figure is, we head over that way." Art said, pointing generally to the southwest.

Jim chimed in, "Ah, Art, I think we should head a little more South than that, what do you think Rayner?"

"Well, Jim, I think you're right. We seem to have been drifting to the right around those hills back there and maybe should correct the course back that way. Or better yet, since I used to be pretty good at cutting sign in the Border Patrol, let me go a couple of hundred yards back and see if I can find our tire tracks. But, I don't know, this ground is awfully rocky. I'll be back in twenty minutes, say 5:15, if not, one of you fire off a round so I know where you are. And, I'll fire one to let you know everything's okay."

So, off I went. After about two hundred yards I spotted a set of our tire tracks that at least would point us in the general direction we wanted to go. There was no road or even a lane, just a path. Carefully marking the location, I went back to the vehicle, we mounted up and Art drove to the point where the tracks were. We took a bearing and rode into the setting sun.

One minute we could plainly see the trail, and the next it was nighttime; so much for the sun slowly sinking into the west. We turned the headlights on high beam and slowly crashed through the trees. We must have missed a turn, because suddenly there was no trail to follow, only a solid wall of brush in front of us.

Were we lost? Not one of us macho outdoorsmen would admit to that. Maybe, slightly disoriented, but NOT lost!

So, Jim and I got out with flashlights and started to back track from the truck. Jim yelled, "For God's sake, Art, don't turn off the truck lights. We'll never be able to find you."

After tracking back about a hundred yards, we came to the spot where the trail turned and we hadn't. I stood at the juncture and Jim went back to the truck. After some backing and turning, Art finally got the carryall turned and came back to me. Since the trail was only slightly visible, we decided one of us would walk ahead of the vehicle as a guide.

A quarter of a mile further on, we came to a crossroads or cross trails and had to decide which fork to take. After a short discussion, we decided to take the fork that appeared more travelled when we noticed the left rear tire had gone flat. Crashing through all the brush had caused all of the tires to pick up numerous cactus needles, to the point that they could be mistaken for porcupines. So here we were in the middle of nowhere, with one flat tire already and the other three appearing as though they would go flat at any moment.

Well, first things first. Without too much trouble, we got the tire changed and were ready to go again. No more crashing through the brush, we would definitely stick to the road. Luckily, about ten minutes later we came out on the Chaco highway, so now it was only a choice of which way to go, north or South? While discussing the options, whisssh, a second tire slowly sank on its rim.

As Jim, Jack and my son were changing the tire; I asked Art, "Is there another gas station north of here? I don't think we can risk trying to drive back to Pozo Colorado."

Art grimaced, "Yeah, I think there is one up this direction, but I just don't know how far."

"Great. Just fucking great! Well, we don't have any choice we'll just have to hope we get to it wherever it is. Just take it slow and see how it goes. We definitely need a change in our luck."

After about what seemed an hour of driving slowly with five of us collectively holding our breaths, Art spotted a fluorescent light ahead on the road, and there was the finest looking gas station in the world. *We had dodged another bullet!!* We pulled up in front of the gas pump, and Art blew the horn several times. Finally, an old man, rubbing sleep from his eyes, came out the door and shook his head, "We're closed, come back in the morning."

All five of us got out of the carryall, and the attendant, seeing our guns cried, "Banditos! Don't kill me!!! Take the money! Don't shoot my wife and me.

We finally got the old man quieted down, told him who we were, showed him the flat tires, explained how we got them and showed him a wad of money. It dawned on him that this was a chance to make some big money off the foreigners who were crazy enough to go driving through the monte, so he agreed to fix our tires, sell us some warm beer and fill the gas tank.

When he finished fixing the two flat tires with their numerous holes, we had him pull the spines out of the four tires we had driven in on. If they were going to spring a leak, it was better here than out in the brush somewhere.

As the light from the rising sun dissolved the cover of darkness, we were ready to head back to the ranch, which we determined was about ten klicks back the way we had come. We arrived back at the ranch at about 7 AM. Tired, hot, dirty and hungry.

The first thing we did was rush straight to the last cooler, which we had covered with a blanket the previous day, hoping to keep the last of the beer at least cool, if not cold. We tore off the cover and opened the chest. Thank God for Mr. Coleman!! There was the last case of St. Pauli Girl covered in cold water with little chips of ice still floating around.

After two cold beers, we stripped off our clothes and jumped into the stock tank. It felt delicious. We ignored the algae and the water beetles and just lay back enjoying the cool wetness. Life wasn't so bad after all.

Finally, feeling alive and half human again, we sat down to coffee and sweet rolls before crashing in our hammocks for an early siesta. After lunch, the guys wanted to take one last crack at being big game hunters, so off they marched into the monte. I, on the other hand, decided my son and I would sit around and get to know each other a little better. Greg and I talked about everything and nothing, just enjoying each other's company.

The other guys came back early, empty handed, not having seen a single thing to shoot. Since we were all tired it was decided to have an early meal and sit around sipping Jack Daniels and branch water in the darkness. Again, what a glorious display of stars, Mother Nature provided. It seemed you could reach right out and grab a handful. Even without the moon, the stars provided enough light we could move around without a flashlight. Really kind of eerie.

As I was drifting off to sleep, I thought over what had occurred during our adventure. First, I had real serious reservations about Jack. But, giving him the benefit of the doubt, I decided maybe I should try to spend more social time with him and find out what really made him tick. Maybe he wasn't really a kook. Time would tell.

Then there was the relationship with my son. It was the first time he and I had time together, not necessarily as father and son, but on a more equal basis, like man to man. And lastly, since we hadn't fired our weapons, I didn't have to clean them.

Early the next morning, we were on our way back down the Chaco road to Asuncion with no problems. After a quick pit stop and fill up at Pozo Colorado we made the trip to the ferry at Villa Hayes in short order. Pulling up to the line of vehicles waiting at the ferry, we walked over to the super tienda for a couple of beers while Greg stayed with the truck.

Upon our return to the vehicle, there was another flat tire on the left rear. Having had enough experience at this, we were like a NASCAR pit crew. Art loosened the lug nuts, Greg and I had the jack half way up and Jim & Jack had the new tire out of the back and ready to be mounted. Pop the flat tire off, throw on the new one, start screwing in the lug nuts, while the jack was being lowered and in four minutes time we were ready to roll. Maybe not fast enough for the Daytona 500, but good enough to impress the natives standing around watching us.

Chapter 14

Jack's True Nature

In 1971, when BNDD opened an office in Asuncion, the main goal was to pressure the Paraguayan government to extradite August Ricord, the Latin Connection, to New York City, where he was under Federal indictment for smuggling several hundred pounds of heroin from France through South America to the United States. Though Paraguay did not have an extradition treaty with the US, they had arrested Ricord and then released him under *house arrest*, awaiting a decision by their Supreme Court on what to do with him. As Ricord had a lot of influence with the Paraguayan government, they were hesitating to move forward on the case.

Shortly after I opened the office, I was joined by Jack, who had joined the BNDD in Los Angeles and after his probationary year was transferred to New York City to get some street experience and to develop into a journeyman agent. After two years in NYC he was assigned to Asuncion as my number two agent. Jack was strange, to say the least. Though he had never worked undercover other than to conduct surveillance, he thought he was a cool street operator. His adopted persona was that of a big bad Mafioso. He dressed in a black silk suit, white dress shirt with French cuffs, with no tie and talked tough out the side of his mouth. He looked like he had just stepped out of a B rated gangster movie from the 1940s.

My secretary, Donnie, a petite thirty something wife of an Embassy communicator, was scared of Jack. When I would be out of town, Jack would play the tough guy role with her, pretending to be the Agent in Charge, and ordering her to do odd jobs that made no sense.

After about nine months, while we were having a drink at the marine house during happy hour, Jack beckoned me out to the rear patio and whispered, "You know the bad guys are watching my house every night and are planning to kill me!"

I thought he was kidding. But he continued, "Also, I keep getting strange phone calls at night, and when I answer the phone the caller hangs up." I thought this was strange as Jack didn't have a telephone at his house.

I solemnly nodded and told him, "O-okay... Dick, the CIA Agent, and I will come over to your house tonight and check out what's happening."

Jack lived in an upscale neighborhood in a large new house at the end of a short unpaved street which ended at a local soccer field and there were three other houses on the block. Dick and I arrived at Jack's house after dark to find the front porch lights on, but no lights on in the house. This seemed odd, and both of us drew our guns and slowly approached the front door. Just as I was about to knock, Jack opened the front door a crack and said, "Quick, come on in."

Once inside, Jack led us to the back patio and pointed to a young man walking across the soccer field.

"See, he does that every night about this time and comes back across the field fifteen or twenty minutes later."

I said, "OK, let's be cool and see what happens."

Sure enough, about twenty minutes later the same young man came back across the soccer field eating an ice cream cone. When I pointed this out to Jack, he said "Yeah, he does that every time but it's a trick."

Just about that time, a car turned onto Jack's street and stopped at the next house about a hundred yards from Jack's house. As Dick and I watched two middle aged couples exit the car and walk up to the front door where they were loudly greeted, Jack rushed into the bedroom and returned with a rifle, into which he was racking a round into the chamber!

"Quick!" he said, "They're coming. You two cover the front and I'll hold them off in the back!"

Dick quickly grabbed the rifle from Jack's hand and said, "Jack, let me cover the back with the rifle, I used to be a sniper in the Army. Since you are the target, go hide in the bedroom and Gordon can cover the front door from here in the living room."

Jack said, "That's a good idea, but I'll stay with Gordon in the living room. That way we can hold them off until help arrives."

After waiting a half hour, Dick came in the back and said, "I did a recon down the back yard and they are just having a family party." Dick then unloaded the rifle and handed it to Jack, forgetting to give Jack the bullets. After a quiet drink, Dick and I left. I assured Jack we would have the local police keep an eye on his house and not to be surprised to see strangers in the area.

As Dick and I got back in my car I said, "I thought you told me you were in the artillery in the Army."

Dick said, "Yeah, I was, but being a sniper sounded better." He added, "Do you think Jack will miss the bullets I took out of his rifle?"

Ha! I answered, "He'll probably think the bad guys took them."

We then drove to the Embassy, where I composed an URGENT message to BNDD Headquarters and the Regional office in Buenos Aires explaining what had happened. A week later, Jack was sent to Los Angeles to supposedly testify in an old case and three days later his wife returned to the states. Jack was placed on medical leave and the Department of Labor was processing his disability claims which BNDD was backing. Things returned to normal, Ricord was extradited to New York, a Paraguayan federal Narcotics Squad was established and a US Customs Agent, Dave Jones, was assigned to the Asuncion office.

Chapter 15

Family Vacation

I couldn't believe it. We were finally on our first family vacation since we came to Paraguay. We would have leisurely prepared for this trip, but a week ago we were informed we had to host a grand bien venido (welcome party) for Carlos Rivera, Gordon's new partner. There was no getting out of it. The BNDD Regional Director was adamant that Gordon introduce the new agent to the diplomatic community before we left on vacation.

The reservations had been made in Punta del Este, the Riviera of South America, in mid season, at a fine hotel by the sea. We had four days to pull this off, and everyone had to give their all if we were going to be on the road in time.

Gordon and his secretary had to extend invitations to all embassy executives, the Mil group officers, AID and the local Paraguayan officials and several foreign embassy executives and their spouses. The guest list would number well over a hundred.

Vicky and I sat down to plan the menu. This was not to be a sit down affair. Most embassy functions of this size were done buffet style, heavy on the hors d'oeuvres, a style which I laughingly called "grazing". All the food groups were included. The only difference was they were all cut to bite size or put together as finger food, and everything was consumed standing around the buffet table, a drink in one hand and picking with the other.

Handing my recipe box to Vicky I asked, "Can you take some of my recipes I used back home and make grazing food out of them?"

"Si, Senora. I have already made them often enough, and it will be no problem."

As she went through the cards she also suggested some of the local food items, "We could use the heart of palm cut in small pieces with the "salsa de golf" for a dip, and my sopa paraguaya can be cut into small pieces."

Between us we put together a menu of tasty and colorful food for our huge table. We prepared a list and made arrangements for the next morning's shopping trip.

"Vicky, I think you are going to need help. So call your sister to come and help you for the rest of the week."

About that time I realized we did not have glassware, napkins, or flatware for such a crowd. I quickly made a call to Gordon.

"Hey, I just realized we need glasses and extra linens for this affair. Ask your secretary how and where to get them on such short notice."

"I've already taken care of all the extas. The embassy has contacts for just such a problem. I've ordered them, and they should arrive this afternoon. I also made arrangements for four bartenders and waiters as well as a guard to handle the parking and security. Oh, and to help with crowd control at the bar, I ordered a satellite bar for the area by the pool."

As I relaxed a bit by the phone I thought. Wow, that takes care of the big *things, now all I have to do is get the house in order, convince the children to help and enjoy the party, and get the packing done.*

The children really surprised me by their reactions when I asked them to help with the party.

"Great. A party! Can we go too?"

"Yes, you can go but this is a formal affair and you will have to dress up and be good!"

They all ran to their rooms to pick out the clothes they would wear to the grand party. At party time, Georgie, who was almost 16, wore a floor length plaid skirt with a long sleeved white blouse. She had applied light makeup and tied up her curled long blond hair with a black bow. Greg sported black dress pants and a white shirt with a string tie. His shoes were also shined. Jo had on a long skirt, like her sister, with a colorful sweater. They were prim and proper as they paraded in front of me for inspection and to get their instructions.

"You can mingle and serve during the party. Remember to say "Yes Sir" or Yes Ma'am". Don't get funny or overly friendly with those guests you know; this is a business affair. Do not run! Walk. Listen to Vicky, and she will give you items to be served. When not serving, you can sit quietly to observe and listen.

The day of the party arrived, the table was laden with food, the bars were stocked with drinks, and everyone was dressed to the nines. The maids and bartenders were on station. All was in order.

Ten minutes before the appointed hour Gordon called out, "Carlos! Now is your time to shine. Get yourself over to the door and get in line. You can't hide. You are the honored guest and you must be part of the receiving line."

Gordon was first in line to welcome the guests and introduce them to Carlos. I was third in line to welcome the guests to our home. Things went smoothly as the guests flowed through the door. There were oohs and aahs about the food and friendly conversation wafted through the rooms and around the pool.

The Ambassador and his wife arrived sociably late, stayed about twenty minutes, shook hands around the room before he made their excuse and left. Gordon and I noticed the noise and lilt of the conversation rose as the remaining guests began to relax and enjoy themselves in the now less formal atmosphere.

I was very proud of the children who performed admirably as they served hors d'oeuvres and made small talk with the guests.

Our quickly thrown together party was a success.

Vicky and her sister were in charge of the clean up and the family finished up the packing to be ready to leave in the morning.

Our goal for the day was to drive to the ferry at Pilar, cross into Argentina and drive to Mendoza, which would put us well on the way to Uruguay.

~~~

Finally, we were off on our great adventure. The check list was complete. The gas tank was full and all our suitcases were on board. Our diplomatic passports with visas to Argentina and Uruguay, our tourist passports, our Paraguayan diplomatic carnets, four certified copies of our vehicle registration, Argentine Pesos, US Dollars and American Express traveler cheques were in the brief case. I had a list of the names and telephone numbers of the embassies and BNDD in Buenos Aires and Montevideo and the friendly high ranking Federales in both countries in case of emergencies.

I had a membership in the new South American version of AAA with maps, routes and mileage. Also included were four cartons of Marlboro cigarettes and three liters of Johnny Walker for gratuities for Customs officials. There was also my Walther .380 PPK just in case. Waving fond farewell to Vicki we drove down the boulevard.

We arrived in Pilar at about 9 o'clock in the morning and were surprised to find only a short line of vehicles for the ferry. Of course, leaving Paraguay was no problem, ten minutes and 100 Argentine pesos later we were on board for the short 15 minute trip to the Argentine side where we found that there was only a cursory inspection by Customs, and we were on our way south and east toward Resistencia.

About 20 minutes later Ella Mae commented, "You told me the Customs inspection would be thorough and take a long time, but it was a piece of cake."

I nodded and pointed out the large sign *"Federal Inspection Ahead. All vehicles must STOP!"* We had crossed the free border zone and were about to enter the interior of Argentina. Here it did take some time. Open the trunk, whip out the diplomatic passports, hand the Customs officials a carton of US Marlboros and smile. The Customs officials were impressed with our diplomatic passports, and the three page car registration with embossed official seals and red ribbons on it. Well, that and the 100 peso bill tucked on the inside. We quickly collected all of our stamped and restamped documents and again were on our way.

After driving through Corrientes we headed south to Santa Fe and found La Posada del Norte, the hotel the embassy travel service had booked us into. It was four star all the way, spacious comfortable modern rooms, European style baths, a restaurant to rave about and room service to bring the bucket of ice for happy hour.

After cleaning up from the day's trip, we went down to the dining room and were seated in a private alcove. The waiter came with warm fresh baked rolls loaded with rich butter and five bread plates. Since this was Argentina, there was only one choice for us, the local "bife" (prime beef) with papas fritas (French Fries) and a heart of palm salad with salsa de golf. Having been out of the States for over a year, when the two younger children discovered they had genuine Coca Cola, they went wild.

We, of course, ordered a bottle of their deep red Malbac wine, which the region is noted for. Our eldest, Georgie, then indicated to the waiter that he should bring three glasses for the wine and while my mouth was hanging wide open, explained to me that she was fifteen and how I was always saying she was grown up, she should be treated like an adult. What could I say?

The waiter arrived with the wine, uncorked it and offered the cork to me to check the quality. I demurred, nodded to my daughter and said, "Let her approve it first."

With a big smile and a grand flourish, the waiter formally offered the cork to my daughter, who smelled it, examined the texture of the stain and said, "It appears to be drinkable. Let me have a taste." The waiter poured a sample into the goblet which my daughter took, smelled and then took a sip. "This is excellent, you may serve."

My jaw had dropped to the table, when I was finally able to ask, "Where did you learn all of that?"

She smiled, "Well, I am my father's daughter and I've watched you do it all the time."

By the time the entrees arrived, we were in need of a second bottle of wine. Georgie was drinking it like water and my wife and I must have been the wittiest conversationalists in the whole town that night, because every comment we would make my daughter thought was the funniest thing in the world. The other kids just looked at each other and shook their heads. What is this world coming to?

Half way through the excellent filet mignon, a funny expression came over my daughter's face and she said, "I don't think I feel too good."

"Some more wine, dear?"

"Oh, daddy, I'm going to be sick!"

"Adult rule number two. Never, ever get sick at the table. That is completely unacceptable. Let your mother take you to the room. I'll bring up your dessert."

Fortunately, when you are young you can recover quickly, and by the next morning Georgie was a little green around the gills, but was ready to continue on to Punta del Este.

The next morning we took off early and headed east to the ferry across the Uruguay River at Concordia. Unfortunately, there was only one other car at the ferry crossing. So when we got to the Uruguayan side of the river the Customs officials had nothing else to do but screw over the tourists. After ten minutes of hassling with the chief officer and a 100 peso "accommodation fee" for the tax stamps for the documents and passports, it was decided that if I shared my 'contraband ' cigarettes and Scotch as a gesture of goodwill, they would forgo searching my luggage. *Well, when you are in Indian country and the cavalry ain't around you play by the Indian rules.*

The highway south to Montevideo and Punta del Este was a two lane highway, straight and in good condition with very little traffic. There were fences on the sides of the highway which meant no sudden appearances of cattle, horses or other animals on the right of way, so I was soon cruising at sixty miles an hour. I flew over this hilltop and there was a car stopped in the oncoming lane, with the hood up and the driver with his head under it. Unfortunately, he was standing in my lane.

Thank God for anti-lock brakes! I slammed them on, locking up all four wheels, steered over on the narrow shoulder almost in the ditch and slid past the vehicle as the rest of the family screamed in unison. The other driver yanked his head out from under the hood, gave a panicked look and shot like a rocket unto and over the hood of his car. I would never have believed someone could jump like that from a standing start if I hadn't seen it.

Needless to say, I don't remember much else about the rest of the slow and sedate drive we made to our destination, the Palmas del Mar beachfront hotel on the bay, in Punte del Este. Our suite on the third floor overlooked the beach and the view stretched for miles in either direction. Since we had booked the reservations through the Embassy and were paying in US dollars, the rates were embarrassingly low.

After the events of the day, immediately after checking into the rooms I made a bee line to the cocktail lounge and ordered a large dry martini on the rocks with two olives to start happy hour. The drink arrived, with two small olives in the bottom, not to quibble; I took a large sip from the glass and choked. ARRRRGH!!!!

This was not GIN, but straight Martini & Rossi Dry Vermouth.

These people had never heard of a Martini, James Bond style. Well, I finally got it across to the waiter what I wanted. He then got the bartender, who came over to really make sure that was what I wanted. So I followed the two of them back into the bar, and showed the bartender how to make a real martini.

"Just wave the vermouth bottle at the glass and then pour in your premium gin and the ice"

I then graciously tipped both the waiter and the bartender and told them that I would be staying for a week and whenever they saw me to bring me one of these.

~~~

As I awoke, the sun was shining through the open door of the apartment, and I could see millions of little dust gems floating on the broad sun beam that lay across the bed. It was 8:00 AM. What I noticed most was the lack of hustle and bustle in the street, but I could hear the faint sound of the waves lapping on the shore a block away.

After our scary trip through Uruguay yesterday and a late dinner, we all fell into bed after we had unpacked. I knew we would all be up and ready to sprint to the beach to splash and swim in the ocean. We were beach people, and we had not seen a beach in over a year.

After a quick breakfast of dulces and juice, we were ready for a swim. As we exited the apartment, we were surprised to see very few people on the street or on the beach. It was odd, but we continued on our quest for the waves and sand. Greg was the first one in, as usual.

He reacted with a shriek, "Eeeks!!!"

"What is the matter?"

"Eeee. It's cold! Someone must have put ice cubes in the ocean."

It was the summer in South America; the air was steaming, the sand was oven hot, but the water was like ice. This was new to us. In

North America, when the weather was hot, the ocean water warmed up also.

As we sat on the beach, we reviewed our knowledge of geography and recalled the Humboldt currents run north along the coasts of South America bringing the cold waters from Antarctica. There was our answer. We spent most of the week splashing a bit in the water, playing in the sand, and catching rays.

As to catching rays, there was the statue man who held our attention and brought a few laughs. Each afternoon a man appeared on the beach. He was about forty years old, five feet ten inches tall, nicely built, still had most of his hair, and wore short shorts and small canvas beach shoes. He did wear sun glasses but brought no blanket, umbrella, or other beach accouterments. He brought only himself and found a spot to stand usually only a few feet away from us on the beach and remained there for 45 minutes. Every few minutes he would set a pose to the sun to ensure he would tan evenly. For a time he would stand with arms akimbo with his face to the sun, or with his balled fists and arms in an olympic bodybuilder pose with face to the sand. During his stay on the beach he would rotate and present many statuesque poses. After 45 minutes he simply walked off the beach, another shade of tan added to his body.

As he walked away, Georgie covered her mouth and giggled. "Do you think he will be back?"

He did indeed return, daily, and we all looked forward to the entertainment. He must have been well known for his sunning technique as no one else on the beach paid him any mind.

As we returned from a full day at the beach for a shower and nap before dinner, I notice there was much more activity on the streets and in the shops. The town was literally waking up,

We soon got the message, "This is a South American party town. They sleep during the day and party all night."

It was 7:00 PM, and we went looking for a place to eat dinner. Snack shops were open and street vendors promoted their tapas and tacos. However, the fine restaurants would not be open until 9:00 PM. Alas we were in South America, and people eat dinner at 10:00 or 11:00 PM.

My answer to this was, "Just the right time to go shopping and see the town."

Off we went to ooh and aah as we poked around in the curio shops and surveyed the many colorful items in the shop windows. As we strolled through the streets, we noticed the shop lights and street lights come on one by one until the city and sky seemed to be aflame with light. The people also came alive, and music seemed to flow from the bars and nightclubs which lined the streets.

This was the true character of Punta del Este. The night life and partying would go on until five or six in the morning, when the shops closed their doors, the bars served their last drink, and the people took to their beds.

As the family became used to this new life, the children took off and did their own thing, and we met for dinner in the evening.

Mid-week Gordon suggested, "Since I am in the area, I should visit with Ralph Saucedo. He runs the office in Montevideo and I would like to see how he is managing. Would you like to go with me? I think the kids can manage on their own."

"Sure, why not?"

When we arrived at the Montevideo office, Ralph and his wife met us. As he introduced his wife he said, "Since Gordon and I are going to talk shop, I thought you and Mary could spend some time seeing the sights in our town."

"Gee, Mary. That would be great. What do you have in mind?"

We spent a few hours strolling through the shops until our feet grew weary, and we began to look for a good people watching spot. That was when we saw an announcement on the window of Stern's Jewelry store. There was to be a seminar on precious stones from 11:00 to 12:00. It was free and no reservations were needed.

We both agreed, "What a perfect place to rest our feet and get an education about gem stones at the same time."

We spent an interesting hour learning how gems were formed, mined, cut and polished. They explained how one gem stone could be different colors and that the clearer and brighter the color the more expensive they would be.

We met Ralph and Gordon for lunch and talked all through lunch about what we had learned at our seminar. As we walked back to the car, we passed several pawn shops that were aglitter with fine jewelry. The economy in Uruguay had hit bottom in the past year and the U.S. dollar was at a premium.

Mary excitedly pointed to a shop window, "Look there is a beautiful yellow topaz. It's not the smoky kind, but clear. We should check it out."

We entered the shop and asked the clerk to examine the ring. It had a clear unblemished stone set in an empire setting, which was my favorite setting. It even fit when I put it on my finger.

The shop owner, a short stocky round faced Latino, smoothly stepped behind the glassed in four foot high jewelry case. To ensure the sale to these gringos, he became very attentive, and in a melodious voice said, "Senora, the ring is very beautiful. It was brought in yesterday by a woman from Germany and I am sure you would enjoy wearing this ring."

"I do like it. How much is it?"

He told me the price in local currency and with the exchange rate the ring would cost $60.00. With a flourish Gordon laid sixty US dollars on the counter. The owner was pleased, and so was I, as I walked out the door with the ring on my finger.

Down the street at another shop we found one more interesting ring; this one a dark green tourmaline. We went through the same process and paid $40.00 for this one. We also saw a pair of diamond ear rings, but on close inspection we could see the flaw in them. So, no sale.

When we returned to the United States we had an appraisal done of the items we bought in South America. These two rings alone were appraised at just under a thousand dollars. The hour spent in the seminar was time well spent and profitable too.

At the end of the week of sun and relaxation, we prepared for the trip home. Gordon had made reservation to take the overnight ferry from Montevideo Buenos Aires.

When Greg found out we would be on the ferry overnight, he asked, "Will we be sleeping, in the car or on the ferry benches?"

Gordon replied, "Neither. We have two small compartments for the night and we will be eating in the dining area. You don't have to sleep in the car."

"Good, can Jo and I go explore?"

"Sure go to it," and off they went.

I thought. *That should keep them busy for a while.*

The ferry was four stories high and seemed to be as long as a football field. Gordon took off for the bar and to check out the workings of the engine, and Georgie and I just strolled along the railing. The sun was low in the sky and the water, brackish in color, had small ripples over its surface. It was going to be a peaceful ride.

As I looked across the water I saw a large area that looked like a bed quilt made of huge beige squares.

"Georgie, look at that. What could it be?"

As we watched and came closer to the "bed quilt", we determined it was a school of sting rays. There were about thirty of them swimming in formation. Each one had a wing span of about six feet. It was fascinating to watch these huge creatures glide along just six inches under the water and not cause a ripple to show on top.

We arrived in Buenos Aires the next morning and headed for home. The rest of the trip was uneventful. We were well rested and ready to face new adventures in this foreign land.

Chapter 16

El Patron

(Master, Captain, Governor)

We had moved into the large mansion on high ground. It needed a lot of care and we had many social obligations due to being part of the American Embassy. It became necessary to employ more servants. A live-in maid was required not only to care for the family but also for the protection of property. In Paraguay there was no crime against person, but if property was left unattended, robbery was almost a certainty.

Vicky, the live-in maid, who did the cooking, laundry, cleaning and general care of the home did fine until the season changed from winter to summer. This brought hot days after very cool nights. As this happened, condensation appeared on the foot thick stone walls and the tile floors. That required someone to mop the floors and some of the walls almost daily. It was time to hire an assistant for Vicky. She informed us her sister, who was married and had 3 children, was available and could work three days a week and whenever needed, to cover social functions. This worked out fine because she did the heavy cleaning and the ironing. Because her social skills were excellent and she was available on short notice, embassy functions were no longer a problem but something to be enjoyed.

Paraguay's laws mandated that maids be supplied with uniforms, three meals a day, health coverage, siesta time (three hours off in the afternoon because most Paraguayans ate between 8 and 10 PM) and vacation time. We paid Vicky $35 a month; I can't remember now what we paid her sister. As a bonus I would order items through the sears catalog for them as well made clothes were not readily available, Vicky and her sister were usually interested in underwear or clothes for the sister's children.

Because we now lived in this large house on a large piece of land we felt like we were living on an estate. There were many trees and flowers in the huge yard. Power mowers were not readily available in

Paraguay and lawn care was done with machete, hoe, shovel, wheelbarrow, and push mower. Neither my husband nor I were going to wield a machete, so it was time to hire a gardener. I can't remember the cost but the law required that he was to have a meal during his day's work. By now you can tell the help had a nice little lunch circle going and lunch was usually served at 12:30 so they could all sit and watch the soap opera, "Estacion Retiro" on TV. I often sat and watched with them as this provided me with another Spanish lesson.

Gordon's job required him to travel to other countries frequently; while he was out of the country, the US Government supplied a night time guard. He would arrive at about 6 PM and be there until 6 AM. I felt secure until one night there was a storm and I could not close one of the upstairs windows as I was not strong enough to close the window against the strong wind. I systematically checked the grounds near the house and finally found him sleeping in our car. As the wind continued to blow and the rain was just about upon us, I quickly rapped on the window. He slowly awoke, opened the door and began to roll his five foot five obese body out of the car while drawing a gun from his pocket. As he realized who I was he awkwardly returned the gun to his pocket. Hurriedly we both went to close the window and I presume after that he went back to his resting place. This was one employee supplied by the Government that really was not necessary as I slept with a gun next to my bed and I had learned many years ago how to use it.

After having all of these servants, I had to keep up with the Jones. A friend of mine had a seamstress to sew her clothes and her children's clothes. Even though I had made my own clothes and my girls' clothes before we went to South America, I decided to see what she could do for me. I had bought several yards of locally made material which was loosely woven and needed to be lined to hold its shape. I never did like lining clothes. She made two or three items and then I decided I could do my own sewing as I had done in the past.

The time we actually felt like the master was at Christmas time. It was gift giving time and they all anticipated something from El Patron.

Chapter 17

Supporting the Neighborhood

After we moved into the big house, we looked around the neighborhood to discover what was available to the family. To our surprise there was a *"Super Tienda"* (large store) across the street. In my mind this was a misnomer.

The store itself was of wood construction and no more than twelve by fourteen feet in total area. There were windows but there was no glass in them, the entry way had no door but was hung with strings of beads. On entering I noticed the floor consisted of red-packed clay and the store keeper was busy sweeping it for the day. The open shelves made of rough 2 x 4 lumber held baskets of oranges, bananas, breadfruit, other small fruits, nuts and vegetables. There were several hammocks hanging from the ceiling in which coconuts, papaya, melons and other large fruits were displayed. On a small shelf were displayed cigarettes and hand-rolled cigars as well as chewing gum.

The family, who owned the Super Tienda, was very friendly and readily available to serve the gringos who had just moved in across the street. This was a bit different than living on the Mexican border where gringos were discriminated against by being ignored or served last. The women were dressed in lose fitting tee shirts and flowing skirts printed with large brightly colored flowers; the men wore cotton pants, rolled to the knees, with very bright colored shirts. I noted they were either barefooted or wore the local huarache sandal. In either case their feet were covered with the red dust from the clay floor. Local music blasted from the radio and seemed to envelope the whole store. There was also a pesky little black-and-white dog that would run to welcome anyone who entered the store.

After settling in, Vicky visited around the neighborhood and when she returned she cheerfully announced, "There is a family living behind us who raise chickens and there is another family in the next block, which has fruits and vegetables for sale. I feel we should buy whatever we can from our neighbors."

"Yes, I think so too. This will make us part of the neighborhood."

The other means of buying local were the colorful street vendors who came by the house balancing full baskets on their heads, calling, "Strawberries, bananas, candy, melons for sale." After the sale was made they would go singing down the street to the next house.

Then there were the salesmen who drove up to the gate in an old rickety truck. Their dress was somewhat more businesslike. They usually wore a dark printed shirt, not tucked in, the sleeves rolled to the elbow and the front closed with perhaps three buttons. They wore dark trousers and real shoes.

They were selling rugs, art work or stainless kitchen ware. They always asked, "Es la senora aqui?" *Is the Lady here?*

I always enjoyed looking at all they had to offer although I knew the items probably had been smuggled into the country. I did break down one time and bought a three piece set of stainless steel cooking vessels which I used for many years after we left Paraguay.

Chapter 18

Medical Emergencies

As the Med Evac plane flew out of Asuncion, I anxiously questioned my friend, "What is wrong with him?"

"They said he had the Amoebas and he needs a complete blood transfusion in order to treat it."

"That's the second one of our embassy personnel this year who had to be flown back to the states. We must be the sickliest people on earth."

The fact that I was a Registered Nurse was always an asset for our family, but never more than the time we spent out of the country. Most of the Embassies had a medical officer who would treat patients with family illnesses or broken bones. However if there was something unusual that required lab studies or a consult for further care any patient in South America was flown to Gorgas Hospital in The Panama Canal Zone or back to the United States. For unknown reasons, the Embassy personnel rarely had insignificant problems but would have life threatening illnesses that required them to be "Med Evaced" out of the country.

I was one of those who might have been sent to Gorgas, but chose not to go. One afternoon I began to have an annoying rhythmic gastric pain which lasted for 24 hours. Nothing I did made it better.

Two nights later I lay in bed thinking, *"I have no temp - not appendicitis, I have no ulcer - pain not relieved by eating or drinking, not a gall bladder problem-no reaction to fatty foods."* Of course Gordon was back in the US for trial and would not be back for a week.

We were fortunate to have a Baptist missionary hospital in Asuncion and the next day I went to see one of their doctors who was as puzzled as I was with my symptoms. He prescribed belladonna drops, a smooth muscle relaxant, to see if that would relieve the continuing rhythmic pains. The medication did not work, and the doctor decided to do a barium swallow and an upper GI study.

The prep and upper GI Study went as expected and as the

technician was looking at the x-rays he asked, "What did you eat last?"

I replied, "Soft cooked eggs, toast and tea."

His reply was, "Well I guess you have an egg shell caught in your esophagus an inch or two above the stomach. That explains the rhythmic pains. Every swallow causes the shell to move. I think it is embedded in the side of the esophagus."

I knew the only way to get to it was by esophagoscopy. Now I had to decide where this would be done. If I went to Gorgas Hospital the children would be alone as Gordon was not due back for a few days.

I asked the technician, "Do you have a doctor here who can do this procedure?"

He replied, "Yes. In fact the director of the hospital is a thoracic surgeon from America."

I did not ask further and made plans to have the procedure done the next morning. Dick Smith, a co-worker from the Embassy, would take me to the hospital and pick me up that afternoon and his wife would check in on the children. This was not a life threatening procedure and everything should be OK by morning. Anyway, so I thought, going in.

Three hours later as I was waking up I knew I would not be walking out of the hospital as I had planned. Every breath I took caused severe pain. The doctor was called. He took one look at me, got out his trusty stethoscope, slowly and carefully listened to my chest and back, then announced, "We need to place a chest tube to drain off the fluid which has collected in your chest."

Evidently the egg shell had worked itself half way through the esophagus wall and its removal had left an opening. Any fluid that I swallowed was going into my chest. The surgeon elected to put me on tube feedings and IVs and wait for the opening to close.

That night the family was scheduled to call my father on the short wave radio. Knowing my seventy year old father would be worried if he did not hear from us, I called my daughter and told her, "Ask Dick Smith to drive you to our radio contact. You and the kids have to talk to Grandpa. Tell him I am in the hospital but will be out shortly. There is nothing to worry about." Needless to say, the children grew up quickly that night.

A day later Gordon arrived home and asked Vicky, "*Donde esta La Senora* (where is my wife)?" She answered, "In the hospital."

"Who is she visiting?"

"No one. She is **in** the hospital."

When Gordon arrived he found me in bed with a feeding tube in my nose, an IV in my arm and a vacuum tube from my chest draining into a bottle on the floor. I sure was a sorry sight to come home to.

I was having other problems also. Any time I tried to sleep, I had dreams or hallucinations of psychedelic colored walls coming in on me. I was also perspiring profusely and needed to have the sheets changed every three hours. This went on for three days and nights. Thank goodness for Gordon. He was there every night changing the sheets and cat napping as best he could on a chair. When the day shift came on, he went home to see the children off to school before going back to work at the Embassy.

The doctor finally took me off the pain killers; the hallucinations went away and the perspiring ceased. Those pain pills evidently were the cause of my problems. I just could not understand why people would pay good money to take pills that leave them in such a state.

The hole in the esophagus closed up, the IV was removed, the chest tube was removed and I finally had a full bath. I felt human again. One good thing came of it. I lost weight and I was down to 112 lbs. To celebrate Gordon took me out for a banana split.

Everyone else in the Embassy said they now chewed their soft cooked eggs.

The next year I cut my arm on a glass shelf in the bathroom. Back to the hospital I went. Since I was now well known at the hospital the intake nurse asked, "What doctor do you want?"

I told her, "It doesn't matter as long as he can sew."

The wound was sutured; antibiotics were prescribed and I returned home. A few days later I began to see haloes around all the lights. Luckily, I had brought my PDR (Physician's Desk Reference) with me. I checked on the antibiotic I was taking and found the doctor had ordered a double dosage. I took one pill instead of two and all the haloes went away.

The moral of the story is when in the Foreign Service one has to look out for one's own medical well being.

Chapter 19

Undercover Work

Being a Narcotic Agent means long periods of boredom,
interspersed with moments of stark terror!!!

Much of my work as a Federal Narcotics Agent was boring and
tedious. It involved long hours of leg work, checking telephone
numbers, freight invoices, hotel receipts or any other kind of data logs.
The information found by cross references or commonalities helped
tie suspect drug traffickers to one another.

Stake outs on alleged stash houses, rendezvous meetings and
photographing suspects going and coming from these places in order
to gain corroborating evidence for a search warrant or an arrest
warrant was not much more exciting than playing a game of solitaire.
Of course, doing surveillance under hostile conditions which could
include the presence of guard dogs or armed counter surveillance, did
raise the thrill level somewhat.

The most exciting and orgasmic thrill was executing an arrest or a
no-knock search warrant on a known violent or armed defendant.
Wow! There was nothing like rushing up to a building, guns drawn and
kicking down a door screaming "Federal Agents with a warrant!!!"

Depending on the reaction of the defendants, such as physical
resistance or gunfire, the thrill meter went off the chart, comparing
favorably to an adrenalin rush. Unfortunately, this was not an everyday
occurrence so I had to settle for the second best option which was
working undercover.

Working undercover is the only area of Federal law enforcement
in which you convince the violator to commit the crime with you or in
your presence. This means you must convince him you are also a
criminal and that he is making a profit from doing business with you.

An undercover deal (U/C) typically starts when an informant
introduces an agent to a suspect. The agent works to gain the suspect's
trust, thus, giving the agent the opportunity to observe the suspect
commit the crime of selling or buying illegal drugs.

Another undercover role is for the agent to provide a service to the violator, such as having the facilities or logistics to smuggle large quantities of drugs into the country. This could include providing small boats to bring the drugs ashore, providing an off-load site, (dock or airport), an off-load crew or a stash house to store the drugs for distribution. Of course the trick is to assure the drugs are confiscated and the dealers are arrested.

Doing U/C work in a foreign country is strictly limited and must meet one of two criteria. (a) As a training tool for local law enforcement or (b) the violator has a direct link to smuggling drugs into the United States or the potential to do so. One of the reasons for these restrictions was that most foreign countries operate under the Napoleonic Code which states that any participant in a crime is guilty thereof, ergo an agent provocateur is also guilty of the crime.

But when things got boring around the embassy, agents looked for ways to stretch the guidelines and conduct a U/C operation. Thus the following:

One day my informant Cambio came into the office and said he had made contact with an Argentine, who claimed he had a source that could deliver multi-kilo quantities of cocaine. This immediately got my attention until Cambio stated that the violator wanted to do the deal across the river in Pilar, Argentina.

Although Pilar is only an hour's drive from Asuncion, it was a small rural town with a minimal law enforcement presence several hundred kilometers from Buenos Aires or any major city in Argentina. I instructed Cambio to go with the Argentine to Pilar, meet with his source, attempt to get a sample of the cocaine, and find out the prices and the quantities that were available.

The following morning, El Gordo, my other informant came to my office and advised me he had watched Cambio meet with the Argentine and that the two of them had taken the bus to Pilar. Things were certainly looking up.

The next day, Friday, Cambio and El Gordo were back in my office, where Cambio told me about the trip to Pilar.

"I met with the Argentine. We took the ferry to Pilar and went to the Hotel de Norte where he introduced me to this woman. She was about forty five years old, five foot six inches tall and weighed 135 pounds, with beautiful shining black hair flowing down her back. She was dressed in a leather outfit like a successful rancher, and introduced herself as Senora del Norte. She told me she had a source for cocaine directly from Chile, and could handle 10 kilos of pure per month at a price of $10,000US per kilo.

When I asked for a sample, the woman laughed and said she would only deal with the main man, not some small time front man. I said I would be back in touch when my 'patron' was in Asuncion the next time. I then took the bus back to Asuncion."

As things were slow on this Friday, I immediately wrote up a cable for Buenos Aires and Washington describing the preliminary steps we had taken and sent it off before going up to the Marine House for happy hour that afternoon.

About noon time the following Monday I received a phone call from Frank, the RD, asking for more specifics and details on this mysterious woman.

"Jesus, Frank, I don't know any more than I wrote in the cable. Is she a hit in the system or what?"

"She isn't a hit in our files, but the Christians In Action (CIA) was standing at my door this morning when I got in. They are very, very interested in her."

"That's neat Frank, but if we try to do a number in Pilar, what kind of Argentine Police backup would there be. This place is a one horse town, out in the middle of nowhere. I don't think there are 500 people there. It's only a ferry crossing."

"Yeah, I know, but to keep our friends happy see if you can push the case along. You know, go meet her, talk shit to her, and get some pics and a phone number. You know things like that."

"Frank, this ain't Boston or Detroit. This is nowhere, Argentina."

"Well, do the best you can and keep the Christians in the loop. Talk to you."

This was getting interesting. Here I am accredited to Paraguay, going across to Argentina to negotiate a multi kilo cocaine deal in a one horse town without any police backup or even telling the police about it. As a gringo, I would stand out like a neon sign.

It made the hairs on the back of my neck stand up. I walked down the hall to the Christians' office and invited my counterpart to go to the cafeteria for coffee.

After getting our coffees and dulces, we found a table in the corner, sat down and I said, "What the shit is going on? Why are you guys interested in a cocaine trafficker way out in the weeds in Argentina?"

"Don't you know about the Montonaros?"

"I know about the Tupemaros in Uruguay, but I never heard of these. What did you call them? Mountineros or what?"

"Jesus, Gordon, you can't be that dumb. Doesn't your agency brief you guys about the terrorists or contras or revolutionaries you might run into overseas?"

"I guess not. Who are these people?"

"Well, you know when you go to Buenos Aires and you see all of those police patrols downtown, you know, the two guys with H&K submachine guns and the third with a big ass German Sheppard. That's because of the Montonaros, the crazy revolutionaries. Besides kidnapping rich people for ransom and blowing up government offices, they do walk up shootings of policemen right in downtown BA during the day time. Things like that."

"So do you think they're selling coke to finance their operations?"

"My friend. That is what you are going to find out. No, actually it would throw a whole different light on their organization if they are. If you can just meet with this bitch and find out if she is for real as a doper or not would be great for us."

"Gordon Rayner, Narcotic Agent Extraordinaire, saves his country!!! Ta Da."

"Yeah, something like that, but don't get yourself hurt, and keep me up to date on what you are going to do."

"Hah, I couldn't keep a secret from you if I tried. You guys read all my cable traffic anyway."

"Yeah, but it would be better on this if you tell me ahead of time. That way I can always send a search party out if you don't come back."

"And the horse you rode in on, buddy."

Two days later, Cambio showed up at the office and I instructed him to find his Argentine connection, go across the river, again meet with La Senora del Norte, and persuade her to meet with me in Asuncion, at least for preliminary negotiations.

The next Tuesday morning, El Gordo came to the office and said that Cambio and the Argentine front man had left on the bus for Pilar and they should be back late that night.

El Gordo, shaking his head, said, "Sr. Rayner, there is something about this whole deal that isn't right. It is bad business."

"Yeah, Gordo, I agree this thing sucks and if it doesn't work out today, we'll just drop the whole thing and just finger this Argentine to the new local narcotics squad. That will give them something to work on. Anyway when Cambio gets back, why don't the two of you come to the office and we'll see what else you two may do for us."

"Hasta mañana, Sr. Rayner. We'll see you tomorrow."

At about 8 PM that evening, I was sitting in the living room reading an adventure novel, when the doorbell at my front gate rang and rang and rang. Someone was really anxious to get my attention. Vicki, who was still in the kitchen watching TV, came out mumbling about those fatherless peons that would bother people this late at night.

I jumped up, grabbed my S&W, jacked a round into the chamber and whispered to Vick, "I'll answer it, when I get to the front door; you turn off the lights, go upstairs and tell the Senora to go to plan C while I go see who is there."

"Si senor, be careful."

I slid out the front door in a crouch and slowly eased across the yard towards the front gate, my S&W held in the two handed combat grip, ready to crank off a few rounds. *Christ, why didn't I take the Embassy's offer for a security guard!!*

As I approached the gate, I heard two familiar voices.

"Oh shit!" It was Cambio and El Gordo. *What were they doing here at this time of night? How did they know where I lived?*

Well, anyway it wasn't a threat, so I flipped the safety on my S&W, and walked to the gate. In a voice that I hoped didn't show my anxiety, I said, "Hola amigos, what are you doing here this late at night?"

"Oh, Sr. Rayner, we must talk to you right away, you are in danger!" Cried El Gordo.

"Okay, okay, take it easy. Come on in the house. We'll talk there."

We went into the front room and I announced in a loud voice, "You can stand down Mrs. R, its' just the CIs." As one of our prearranged signals, if I had called her Ella Mae, she would have known there was a problem, but calling her Mrs. R meant everything was okay.

The three of us walked down the hall to my office, past the doorway to the kitchen, where I glanced out of the corner of my eye and saw Vicki hiding against the wall with a massive butcher knife clutched in her hand.

"Vicki, its' alright these are friends."

When Cambio, El Gordo and I were seated in the library, I asked, "What's the problem? Cambio, I've never seen you this nervous, what happened? Can I get you a drink or coffee or some water?"

"No, thank you Sr. Rayner, but I must tell you what happened today in Pilar. When the Argentine and I crossed the river, we went to the cantina in the hotel and he told me to wait there and someone would come to take me to see the Senora. He then went out the back door and disappeared. I never saw him again."

"Then what happened?"

"I was the only one in the cantina and about twenty minutes later, a tall man in rough ranch clothes came in and said I should follow him.

We went out the back door into an alley and two other guys jumped me. One stuck a gun in my side and said he would kill me if I made any noise. The other threw a sack over my head and tied my hands behind my back. I kept saying that I was only a poor business man and didn't have any money. I thought they were going to rob me."

The tall guy laughed, "Be quiet, fool, we are going to take you to see La Senora."

"I heard a car pull up and stop. They picked me up and threw me in the back seat with two big men, one on either side of me. We drove out of town on a rough country road for about fifteen minutes. The longer we drove the bumpier the road became. We finally came to a stop in a farm yard. They dragged me out of the car and into a poor one room shack where they sat me roughly in a chair. No one said anything for a long, long time. Maybe a half hour or more. I was very scared. The only sounds were the chickens and goats in the yard and my own breathing. I didn't even know whether they were still in the room with me, but I was too frightened to even move.

Finally, one of them said, "She's coming. Take the bag off his head, but don't untie his hands. We will wait for her orders."

I heard a car door open and slam shut and a woman's voice ask where I was. Shortly, she entered the doorway, but in the bright light I couldn't be sure if it was the woman I had met before. She stood in front of me, hands on her hips, and said, "Oh, the little man has come back. He must really want to do business with us."

"By this time, my eyes became accustomed to the light and I could see four men with machine guns, standing behind the woman. Sr. Rayner they looked like very rough banditos."

"Here is the deal, Mr. Cambio. We know you are an informant for that American Narcotics Agent in the embassy. We want you to go back and tell him you have seen the cocaine here in Pilar and we will sell it to him for a very low price, but it must be in Argentina. Tell him to bring some money with him, so we know he is for real and we will do the business.

When we get him here we aren't going to kill him, but we are going to hold him for ransom, he should bring us a good price, probably better than most of these ranchers and business people we have to work with here.

Whatever Sr. Rayner is paying you, I promise we will pay you much more. Once we get the Yankee money we will pay you $10,000.00 US. If you try to trick us, you and your whole family will be killed as a warning to those Yankee capitalist dogs, and we have many ways to hurt you. It will not be pretty and we will let you watch us torture and rape your wife and daughters before we kill them. Even the little one, the ten year old."

"Oh, I was so scared that I wet my pants and promised her I would do what she wanted me to do, but I wasn't sure I could convince you to come here. I told her what you had said about having to do the business in Asuncion and not here in Argentina."

"She became very angry and said, "You should try very, very hard Sr. Cambio. Don't forget what I said about your family. We are everywhere and know what goes on in that dirty capitalist embassy. Viva la revolution!!""

"She turned, walked out, got in the car and drove away. None of the men said a word, though two of them looked like they wanted to kill me. You know, they had those mean hard eyes. Just like you do."

"About an hour later the car came back and they put me in the back seat, covered my head and drove me back to Pilar, where they pulled into a side street, cut loose my hands, snatched the hood off my head and kicked me out of the car. I was finally able to get my directions straight and went to the ferry to come right back to Asuncion. I went to El Gordo's house and we came right over here."

"That's quite a story, Cambio. You and El Gordo go home, and tomorrow, after you have recovered, come to the Embassy and we can go over this again. There are some other people who should hear this story."

"Thank you, Sr. Rayner. Oh, one other thing, her name is not La Senora del Norte, but is La Senora del Muerte!!!"

~~~

About two months later, we had a Regional meeting in BA with Gary Sticker, our control from Headquarters. I told him briefly about the Montonaro kidnapping attempt and asked him if our Agency had a line item in the budget for paying ransoms. He looked at me straight faced and with a slight smile said, "Sure it's' ten million dollars, but don't get kidnapped in September. You know the budget runs up to October first, so any funds that are not spent by the beginning of September, we reallocate to other line items.

Well, look Mr. Kidnapper, you're going to have to wait until the first of the month to get paid.

Chapter 20

The Friday Night Poker Club

Things at home were slow. The boxes were unpacked but there were still odds and ends setting around on the tile floors waiting for a permanent location on the wooden mantel or to be hung on one of the bedroom walls.

I decided it was just the time to take a break and visit Gordon's office in the embassy to see where he worked when he was in Asuncion. It was a warm sunny day; just right for walking. As we lived only a few blocks from the embassy I decided to walk.

As I strolled by the front of the neighboring property I was jolted out of my tranquil frame of mind. There was a big snarling German shepherd running along beside me in the yard. The yard was raised about three feet above the pavement, putting the barking mouth of the dog almost at eye level. I didn't know whether to run or just give up and die. The dog didn't come at me, just ferociously ran back and forth on the property line. What was most amazing was the fact that the three foot wall was topped by only a single two inch pipe and the dog could easily have launched himself over it any time, but he didn't. Well so much for my nice stroll for the day. It took me the few blocks I had to walk to get my nerves under control again.

As I entered the embassy the Marine Guard, nattily attired in his dress blues, asked, "What is your name and what is your business at the embassy?"

I gave him my name and told him, "I am here to check out my husband's office. He is the new DEA officer."

"That's fine ma'am. The office is on the second floor, second office on the left."

I introduced myself to the secretary who showed me into Gordon's office. I was impressed as it had a nice big window, two desks and many file cabinets. In his prior positions he shared an office with several agents and there was one secretary to keep up with all of their case work and filing.

As Gordon and I were commenting to each other how things had changed, Art Kohl, the commissary manager, sauntered into the office. He was on a mission. He was looking for a fifth for the Friday night poker game. He complained, "Two of the guys are out of town and I found one substitute but I don't know who else to call."

I smiled coyly and said, "I'll play if you really need someone."

He looked at me in disbelief and really didn't have the nerve to say he didn't want a woman playing in their men's poker club. I could just read it on his face. He stammered a bit and said, "Well. Ah. Gordon. I'll get back to you later."

As he left I quietly said, "I could wear my green eye shades and wear garters on my shirt sleeves if that would help the image."

He huffed and kept on going.

On Friday night we both went to Happy Hour at the Marine house and had a drink with Art. He was still searching for his fifth player.

Gordon with a sly grin told him, "My wife is still available to play."

Art shrugged his shoulders and said, "OK, you can bring her if you want."

Gordon and I smiled to each other. This was going to be like old times. While he was in college we had very little money for entertainment so the neighborhood couples got together to play penny ante poker. If we lost three dollars it was time to go home.

We arrived at the designated home at 7:00 PM where Art quietly made the introductions and explained, "I couldn't find a fifth because everyone is out of town or busy. Gordon's wife said she would fill in."

As we took our seats around the dining room table covered by an old army blanket, I slowly studied the other players. Art was a former marine who had retired in Paraguay to marry a local girl. He was about 45 years old, six feet tall, clean shaven with sandy blond hair, of muscular build, wearing chino pants and an open plaid shirt with rolled up sleeves and very sure of himself.

Don, the number two admin officer of the embassy, was five feet ten inches tall, overweight by fifty pounds, and wore a dark blue suit with a white dress shirt open at the neck. He appeared much laid back and on the quiet side. The fact that he was on his second drink probably attributed to his demeanor.

On the other hand there was Jim, a communications specialist, who was bubbly and full of life. A red-faced Irishman in his mid forties, wearing horn rimmed glasses and a knowing smile, surely believed I was easy prey and he would cash in on this game.

Drinks were served and we took our seats. The rules were explained: The game is over at ten; bets are in guaraní, the local currency; five guaraní ante and ten guaraní bets or raises until a pair is showing. With a pair showing you could bet twenty five guaraní with a three raise limit.

The room was full of cigarette smoke, cards were dealt and the game was on. I picked up my cards and after the draw I was holding a full house. The bets began and the raises went to the limit. Low and behold there were three of us holding a full house. Mine was not the winning hand, but I held my own and much to everyone's amazement they did not have to tell me how to play the game. Gordon and I just smiled as we picked up our cards for the next deal.

As you can surmise after that night I was part of the Friday night poker club as long as I came with Gordon. A few months later, when Gordon was out of town on one of his undercover deals, I received a call from Art, "Are you coming to the poker game this week?"

This was unexpected and I was not sure how to answer. Since I was the only woman in this club, I was a bit concerned about the opinions of the other wives if I attended on my own. I told Art, "I don't know, I'll get back to you." A few days later I received a call from Don's wife who said, "The poker game is at our house and the boys would like you to come to the game. I will be serving drinks and food if you were concerned about coming alone."

I said, "OK, I'll be there."

However to cover all the bases I did ask my ten year old son, Greg, to come with me and told him to go to sleep on the couch if he got tired. Little did I know then, my son had a photographic memory and he would grow up to be a card shark.

Chapter 21

The Imported Christmas tree

After our first Christmas without a tree, I was determined to have a tree for our next Christmas in Paraguay. I mulled over possible solutions in my mind.

I can't use a tree from here. No pine trees in sight. Darn it, I have to use a palm tree. Nah, I will not do that. I have to think of something.

All the embassy personnel had relatives back in the states that sent them care packages on a somewhat regular basis. These packages would include personal items such as tooth paste, underwear, magazines, news papers and above all toilet paper. The only toilet paper available in this country felt like a rough paper towel. Ouch!

A bright idea, "I know how I will do it! I will have my tree." We had already received several such care packages through the APO services. The APO mail did not have to go through customs and was delivered directly to the Embassy which meant there would be no import duties applied.

An artificial tree could be broken down and packed into two or three boxes to be sent by APO. These trees were not too heavy so the cost couldn't be too much. I was dancing around the library with pictures of a lighted Christmas tree glowing in my mind as I decided to ask my brother, Luther, to purchase a tree and send it.

Since we arrived in Paraguay, we had been making monthly calls to my father by shortwave radio and Luther would accompany my father to the home of a short wave operator in Pennsylvania. This made the request easy, or so I thought.

During the radio call I talked to my brother and asked, "Luther, do you think you could buy me an artificial tree, repack it and send it to me? Over."

He said, "Yah, I guess so. Where do I send it? What kind do you want? Over."

"Get a medium sized one and one that looks like a pine tree. Not one of those aluminum ones. Send it to our APO address. Daddy has the address. I'll send you a check for $60.00 to cover the cost and mailing. Over."

We finished the call to my father and went home to anxiously wait for my tree to arrive.

A few weeks later Gordon received a call at the office. It was from Paraguayan customs saying, "Senor, your package is here. You can pick it up and you owe customs $120.00."

Gordon angrily called me, "Didn't you tell your brother to send *your* tree APO? And do you want to know what it is going to cost us?"

At this point there was not much we could do. Gordon paid customs and brought home a large fragile box that contained **my** Christmas tree. My brother had never repacked the tree into smaller boxes; he had just slapped an address label on it and sent it by Air Mail. I was really upset with Luther but I had my tree.

With great anticipation I unpacked the tree from the box and put it together branch by branch and was thinking to myself.

This tree has cost us a lot of trouble and a lot of money and we are going to enjoy it. Since it is the only Christmas tree around, everyone in the Embassy is going to enjoy it too."

American Embassies provide furnished homes to assigned personnel; therefore we did not bring any of our furnishings with us such as Christmas decorations for the tree. I told Vicky and the children, "We have to put our heads together and be very creative. This tree is going to be unique. It is the only one here."

A care package arrived with two strings of Christmas lights and a pack of tinsel. I shopped down town for construction paper to make colorful chains as well as different designs to hang among the branches. A package of popcorn bought at the Embassy commissary provided the children and me a few days of entertainment popping and stringing popcorn to drape around the tree. Many years ago we had learned to make origami birds; many of those origami doves nested in our tree. We also baked and decorated sugar cookies. We were finally ready for our Christmas tree to make its debut.

There were several dinner parties for our close friends to view and enjoy the grand sparkling Christmas tree, probably the first of its kind in Paraguay. We also put an invitation on the bulletin board at the Embassy and the Marine house:

You are invited to stop by to
See and enjoy
The Christmas tree
Gordon & Ella Mae Rayner

Many visitors arrived to view the shinning Christmas tree and Christmas was a festive affair compared to the year before.

Chapter 22

A Week At The Cattle Ranch

It was the Christmas season and we were all sitting in the living room enjoying the Christmas tree and imbibing the Commissary booze. Our American friends from the Paraguayan country side were expounding on their adventures as pioneer farmers and ranchers in this primitive country.

Bill piped up, "Why don't you all plan to spend Easter with us on the ranch? Then you can see what we are talking about."

John Shuman and his wife Mary were the farmers. He was a retired Marine Corps Lt. Col. who had bought 200 hectares in the northern part of Paraguay just off the only unpaved road from Asuncion to Pedro Juan Caballero. The land had been cleared for farming and he was growing maize and soy as well as food for the family's use.

Bill Arnold was a retired Air Force Lt. Col. who bought 1000 hectares in the hopes of raising cattle. This land was nowhere near a road and the only way in was by plane or by horseback. The majority of the land was covered by dense jungle that included Lapacho trees the wood of which was very dense and considered a premium product.

Bill told us, "You know a funny thing. I flew my Piper Super Cub from Florida to Paraguay across the Caribbean and down along the east coast of South America and I was seldom out of sight of land for more than a few minutes."

When we had finished off the last of the Harvey Wall Bangers the three families had made an agreement to meet at the cattle ranch for Easter.

~~~

"I have the booze, who has the chocolate?"

"The chocolate is packed in Georgie's suitcase."

"OK, I think we are ready to go."

Everyone in the family was excited to go on this trip because it was going to take us into the interior of Paraguay. Because there were no roads to where we were going we would have to go in by air.

We left Asuncion on a DC-3 for Pedro Juan Caballero. At that time Paraguay was using our old military C-47s for their passenger airlines which to us seemed a bit primitive. The fuselages had not been repainted and were still that dingy military silver gray and the interior was a flat olive drab color. There was no extra cushioning on the seats and there was no stewardess. After two hours we landed at PJC. All of us were anxious to meet our hosts who were to fly us to the ranch in their plane.

It was a bright sunny day in April when we landed in Pedro Juan. We climbed off the plane and hauled all our bags and goodies to the side of the runway and waited for our host to pick us up. There were not many trees around and the fields were covered with tall dry grass.

Greg was impatient, "I hope they didn't forget we were coming."

"I doubt that. We have all those things from the commissary that they are looking forward to."

To the East we saw three Piper Cubs starting to circle in order to land. One by one they landed, rolled by us, circled on the runway and came to line up close to us. They turned off the engines and all was quiet and eventually the dust settled. We all clapped and shouted when they got out of their planes. Bill, our host, had asked two of his neighbors to fly in with him to pick us up so he would not have to make multiple trips. After all he had to ferry five of us, our luggage and the goodies from the Embassy commissary we would need for our week at the ranch.

Bill greeted and hugged us. He moved and sorted our luggage and then assigned each of us to one of the planes.

"Why can't I go with daddy? Instead Jo is going with him." grumbled Greg

Bill very good-naturedly replied, "Well, the plane will only carry a certain amount of weight. I have several bags of supplies I have to take with us and I know what they weigh. So you kids and your mom and dad have to fit into the plane to even out the load."

Georgie Ann and I climbed into the one plane which already had a large burlap bag tied into the front seat. Bill made sure our seat belts were in place then taxied down the runway and in minutes we were in the air. Below us were miles and miles of nothing but green forests with a few rivers here and there and a few trails that looked like crazy footpaths.

After about 20 minutes, I felt the plane descend and in the distance I saw a large white brick building in the middle of a large clearing. Next to the building was a green flat area that I presumed was to be our landing area. The plane lowered and we flew by the house about 50 ft from the ground, but we didn't land.

"What's the matter? I thought we were going to land."

"Yes. We're going to land next time around. I have to clear the area and chase the cows off the runway before we come in."

We finally landed and rolled to a stop. As we climbed out of the plane I was overwhelmed by this huge white brick building in the middle of nowhere. We had just left Asuncion where all the buildings reminded me of the houses in the towns of the old west during the early 1900s. There was just no comparison.

"Bill, how did you accomplish this or where did you get the bricks?"

"While I was supervising the land clearing, I found a deposit of white clay. So I learned how to make bricks and taught the locals. Now I have this house, my own brick maker and am selling the bricks to my neighbors,"

As we went up to the house I estimated it to be about 80 feet wide. It was one story with a wide porch across the front of the house.

The first things I noticed as I stepped into the thirty by twenty foot living room were the fireplaces. There was one at each end and they were big enough for a grown man to stand up in and take three or four steps to the other end. Since there was no electricity available, these fireplaces were the means to heat the house during the cold spells.

On each side of the living room was a bedroom suite and to the back was a large kitchen which opened up unto a covered patio. Beyond it was a pool and an open view of the sweeping green ranchland.

I mentioned earlier that there was no electricity and I was very interested in seeing how heat, water pressure and light were provided for everyday living.

In the living room were two propane tanks with attachments which made them look like floor lamps. They were actually Coleman lanterns. During the day and early evening they were in the living room and at night were moved to the bedrooms.

To the side of the patio I found a windmill which had been built to lift the water from the well into a storage tank on the roof. From there the water was directed through pipes to the kitchen, bathrooms and the pool where the runoff provided water for the cattle.

All I could think was, "I would have to take cold showers." But, no, they had that covered also. There was a large wood burning stove in the kitchen through which they had run the water pipes as well as through the two fireplaces. The water running through these pipes would be warm by the time it reached the showers.

"This week at the ranch wasn't going to be too bad after all."

Gordon's Memories Of The Flight

The flight from Asuncion to Petro Juan Caballero (PJC) was uneventful. As uneventful, as it could be, knowing you were flying in a C-47 of World War II vintage that had been sold by the American government as surplus and only slightly modified by having passenger seats installed.

Upon arrival at PJC, we deplaned, entered the basic terminal that consisted of one check-in counter and one porter who quickly collected our luggage. The kids were all excited. They had flown in U.S. airlines several times, but this was their first experience flying in a twin engine converted cargo plane. The porter started towards the door to get us a taxi.

"Wait," I said, "We are going to be picked up by Senor Arnold in his airplane."

The surprised look on the porter's face was enough to tell me this was not a common occurrence. He then wheeled the baggage cart around back through the arrival doors out onto the tarmac past the parked C-47 and unloaded our bags onto the concrete. I tipped him and he returned to the terminal leaving us and our baggage on the taxiway. *Well, this was getting interesting.*

Shortly, our onward transportation came into view. Three planes circled the airport and landed one after another and taxied towards us. When they shut down their engines, the pilots got out of their planes and came over. I knew Col. Shuman and Bill who introduced us to the third pilot, John West, an American Baptist missionary, who ministered to a flock in a small remote village about 60 miles from PJC.

We soon loaded up and were off to Bill's ranch. It was a half-hour flight, but John related it would take Bill a full day to get there in his four-wheel drive Jeep and that was in dry weather. During the rainy season it was impossible.

After dinner that evening Bill and I went out on their rear patio to watch the sunset. As we sat sipping our Jack Daniels on ice, the sun majestically sank behind the western hills and the sky filled with thousands of stars. With no air or light pollution, the stars were brilliant in their overwhelming numbers. I had never seen the night sky so radiant. It felt like I could reach up and touch them.

As I was soaking up the scene, I looked out over the ranch and saw a small light flickering on a far hillside. "Bill, what is that light? It looks like a far off firefly."

"Oh, that's the oil lamp in my brick maker's house. It's about two klicks away."

"Jesus, that's over a mile and a half!"

"You got it. That's one of the best things about living out here and it's all mine as far as you can see."

The Men's visit to PJC

The next day Bill said, "Since the women are going visiting, you and I can fly to PJC. We have to pick up a few items on the Brazilian side."

After running a couple of steers off the runway, we cranked up the Super Cub, took off, and flew to PJC. Upon landing, we caught a taxi to take us to PJC, Brazil.

Being used to border crossings in Texas and Michigan I asked, "Well, am I going to need my passport or will my carnet from the Paraguayan police suffice?"

"We'll have to wait and see, but I think we can sneak you across."

After a short drive through the Paraguayan side of PJC, we came to an open area about a hundred yards wide stretching out in either direction. On the Paraguayan side was a two-lane concrete street and on the Brazilian side a similar road, but this one had street lights. No fence, no border guards, no traffic control, no immigration or customs inspection, but only a sign in the middle of the street reading "Welcome to Brazil."

I turned to Bill and said, "You've got be kidding. This is all there is?"

"Yep, the real control point in Paraguay is twenty six klicks down the road and it's the same in Brazil. This is what they call the free border zone. How do you think I got all the stuff to build my house? I got it all in Brazil, including the cement, hardware, windmill, appliances and building materials. Everything. Oh, and that includes the craftsmen for the work I couldn't do myself. They even hauled in a portable saw mill to cut the lumber from my Lapacho trees for the framing and floors. That wood is so hard it will last longer than I will. You're going to be surprised at how modern the Brazilian side is, even though it's a long way from any big city. Hell, they even have a paved road from here to the interior of the country."

He was right. The first stop we made was at a modest

supermarket and to my great surprise there was a freezer chest outside the store with ice cream and popsicles in it. This was something I had never seen in Paraguay, not even in the capital. Our next stop was a small, well supplied hardware store that would fit in any small town in the U.S. No wonder most of the people crossing the border were bringing empty bags from the Paraguayan side and returning heavily laden from Brazil.

We flagged down a taxi and returned to the Super Cub, where we loaded all of our purchases into the rear of the plane, climbed in, fired up the engine and taxied to the end of the runway. There Bill asked, "Do you want to take off and fly back to the ranch?"

Surprised, I said, "Sure, just tell me how to do it."

"No sweat, push the throttle forward until the plane starts rolling. Then keep it in the middle of the runway with the rudders and when it feels light, pull the stick back gently and off we go."

Amazingly, that's just what happened and we were airborne.

Bill instructed me saying, "The important thing is keep all of your movements soft and gentle, otherwise you'll roll the damn thing upside down and we don't want that."

"Oh yeah, this is going to be fun!" I groaned, as I held the stick in a death grip and started sweating profusely.

I asked, "Which way do we head to get back to your place?"

Bill pointed ahead and said, "See that road leading west out of town, that's the road to Asuncion. Just follow it and I'll tell you when to turn left onto my road to the ranch."

Sure enough, about fifteen minutes later as we were coming up on the customs and immigration control point, I saw a narrow one-lane track on the left that wound through the forest. It followed the contours of the hills and valleys, crossing small streams and skirting the rock outcroppings, taking the path of least resistance through the terrain. Finally, I spotted Bill's white brick house in the middle of the raw countryside and pointed it out to him.

"Yep, right where it's supposed to be. You better let me take the stick; landing is a little more difficult than taking off. I mean you just showed it don't take much brains to take it off, but it requires a little more skill to land this. See if you can spot any cattle on the runway. I don't want to hurt one that I've busted my ass to raise."

We flew over the runway and seeing it was clear, Bill threw the throttle forward, gained altitude, did a sharp roll over the field and dove towards the end of the strip in a steep dive, flaring out, dropping the flaps, cutting the throttle so the plane softly floated to earth.

"Christ", I said, "that scared the hell out of me." Bill laughed,

"You know I used to fly fighters in the Air Force and once a fighter Jock, always a fighter Jock. Hey, anyway we defied death and destruction one more time."

A Visit To The Neighbor

After a few days sitting around and catching up on each family's adventures, the men left in the plane to pick up supplies in Pedro Juan Caballero. As we waved good-by to the departing plane, Ann said, "Now is a good time for us to visit my French neighbors, Pierre and Francine. Pierre is from Paris and is trying his hand at cattle ranching and Francine, of all things, is the daughter of a French fashion magazine owner. We feel they are a bit naive and are not sure they will last under the harsh conditions here in Paraguay. Their ranch is about twenty minutes away and we will be riding the horses."

Since I was raised on a farm, riding a horse was not a problem. Although I had not ridden a horse for years, I was not sure how I would dress for this adventure. I had not planned on anything like this. Hiking around the ranch and sitting by the pool were what I had in mind when I packed my bag. I put on a pair of blue jeans and my old pair of tie sneakers would have to do. I found a red scarf to tie around my neck and plopped a straw sun hat on my head. I was ready to ride. Hi Ho Silver, here we come!

Ann, a tall well built woman in her late forties, strode out of the house wearing long nicely fitted khaki colored slacks that were tucked into well worn brown cowboy boots. Her red toned plaid shirt had short sleeves and an open collar. To my surprise she had a four inch barrel Smith & Wesson revolver tightly strapped on her right hip. I gave her a questioning look as to why she needed the firepower.

She smiled coyly and said, "We may encounter a rattlesnake along the way and besides the hired help expects *their senora* to wear her pistol whenever she leaves the ranch."

As we walked to the stable, a small one story unpainted wooden building about twelve by sixteen, she explained, "This is where we lived when we first arrived. I was ecstatic to move into the brick house when it was finished."

"I can imagine. This was quite a change for you coming from a home in Washington, DC. How did Bill ever talk you into marrying him and coming to this God forsaken place at your age?

"I guess I was just swept off my feet and I always was a bit adventuresome."

We entered the stable and the reddish colored horses eagerly came to us and nuzzled our hands looking for a treat. They were not work horses like I was used to on the farm but stock horses. They were quite tall as my head was shoulder high to them and they appeared lean and sleek. Their front quarters were slim and taut and the hind quarters bulky and muscular.

I was a bit awed by their size and told Ann, "I think I will need some assistance to swing into the saddle."

"OK. You will find a block by the side of the stable that you can use."

I needed a few tries to get into the saddle. All the while, she assured me she had given me the calmer one.

We started off at a slow trot; the two horses nickered to each other as though they were happy to be out of the stable on an outing. It was a clear fall day. This seems a bit odd to say; but in Paraguay, the seasons are reversed and Easter is in the fall. The air was clear and odorless. Here, there were no cars, factories or rotting food or animals to affect the atmosphere; only green vegetation could be seen covering the countryside.

When we left the cleared area we entered the forest which was green and lush with overhanging tree limbs and the forest floor was covered with green ferns. Only a few small animals scampered among the leaves.

As we rode along I realized there was no road or lane to be followed. Instead we appeared to be following paths that had been made by the animals in the area. Sometimes we circled low around a small rise and the next we were riding over the crest of a hill. It was a quiet peaceful ride and shortly we came out on a small clearing that had a partly constructed house on it.

The majority of the walls were not yet in place and hammocks with mosquito netting were hung from the wall studs. After spending a few nights in the big white brick house of our hosts, this home seemed very primitive.

As we came into the open sided house I noticed very few furnishings. There was a small wooden bench, a wooden table and 2 camp chairs. Francine invited us to sit down on the side of the open porch floor and asked, "Would you like some tea?"

As we chatted she casually set a well used and unpolished silver tea kettle on a Sterno stove to prepare the hot water. As we talked waiting for the water to boil, I looked about and realized there was no regular stove in sight on which to prepare food. She may have had a grill somewhere for cooking but I was not about to ask.

As we chatted about this and that, I observed Francine. She was about twenty seven years old, five feet five inches tall and weighed about a hundred and twenty five pounds, had long dark uncurled lackluster hair, sallow complexion, and her brown deep set eyes showed no spark. I thought to myself, *this lady is not going to last long in Paraguay.*

After about a half hour of talking about the weather, what Pierre was to do on the house, and what we were doing on this visit, we said our good bye and Francine greedily hugged both of us saying, "It is so good to see someone. Do come again, soon."

Our return ride to the cattle ranch was quiet and restful and I thought to myself, *"I sure am lucky to be where I am in life and it is good to get a better understanding of how others live."*

The Night Marchers

It was the end of another fun filled day, the dishes had been washed and put away, a few elbows had been bent and the children had finished their game of Monopoly. Everyone was ready to turn in.

The propane lamps had been moved to the bedrooms and the children had laid out their sleeping bags in the living room. They were chattering away as the grownups each moved to the bedrooms at the opposite ends of the house.

When the propane lamps were doused the light of the full moon filled the rooms. Things were quiet on the home front and everyone drifted off to sleep.

About 2:00 in the morning, Jo came to my side of the bed half crying and scratching her neck and arms saying, "I'm itchy and I feel like something is crawling on me."

Slowly I woke up and took her in my arms to try and calm her down. As I was holding her I also felt something crawling. Then I was really awake. I shook Gordon, "Wake up and turn on the lamp. There is something crawling on Jo!"

By the time Gordon fumbled with the matches and lit the lamp, the rest of the children and our hosts were also awake. More or the children were complaining of crawly things and the lamps were pulled into the living room where we saw what was causing all this uproar.

There was one line of ants marching through the room. They were coming in the back door, through the kitchen and living room and out the front door. Our host said, "Just get out of their way and they will pass through." We brushed off the children and let the ants go on their way."

While we waited for them to be gone, Bill told us about the ant incident at the home of their neighbor. One night their crying baby woke them. When they got to the crib, there were ants all over it and throughout the house. They quickly bundled up their daughter and left the house and ended up spending the night in their truck. They returned to find their house very clean as the ants had eaten anything that was not in closed containers, as well as all insects and roach eggs. They were considered the house cleaners of the area.

After the ants had gone the adults slowly returned to their rooms taking the lamps with them and the children went back to sleep in the moonlight each curled in a chair.

High Stakes Poker Game

Easter morning sunrise was celebrated on the patio with Bloody Marys. As we were planning Easter dinner, John West and his family flew in to share the festivities with us.

Bill was busy preparing our breakfast, when he called to us, "Come see this antique waffle iron I found at a flea market back in the states. I bought it because it fits into the opening of my wood burning stove. See, I can even turn it over as the waffle cooks."

Every one helped prepare dinner. The main course naturally was beef, (Asada Befi`). The sides were mandioca, a local vegetable similar to potatoes, green beans and a salad with palmito (heart of palm).There was also the Paraguayan staple, Sopa Paraguaya. To me it was a glorified corn bread made with cheese, eggs and onions. The dessert was an American favorite, chocolate cake.

The Holiday was coming to an end. The dishes had been washed and put away, a few elbows had been bent and the children finished their game of Monopoly, Bill and John decided the men should play real poker. Gordon, Greg and Bill's son Andre agreed to play but no one had much cash in their pockets and also Greg and Andre were under age. To solve the problem they raided the monopoly game for play money.

The game ran late into the night. Much beer and wine were consumed and at times tensions ran high as the stakes at times were huge. It was amazing to watch three grown men and two boys playing a serious game of poker with play money.

Throughout the week Jo and Greg talked about the outings Andre, Bill's fifteen year old son provided for them. Their adventures through the country side were on horseback. Georgie, who was also fifteen at the time, was smitten by this muscular fine looking young man who was only too happy to escort her around the ranch. When the youngsters were not on horseback they were shouting and splashing in the pool by the patio.

At the end of this relaxing and adventuresome week we had to pack up and return home the way we came. However this time we only needed two planes to leave the ranch as they were only transporting people. The trip home was uneventful but our minds were filled with many good memories.

Chapter 23

Quito, Ecuador

In April, 1973 Dick Heath, the Agent-In-Charge in Quito, Ecuador was doing an undercover job in Curacao, Netherlands Antilles, when he was shot in the left thigh by a defendant during the arrest. He received minimal treatment on site and returned to Quito. A week later a blood clot broke loose from the wound and caused his death.

Three weeks after Dick's death, I was called to Buenos Aires (BA) to meet with the Regional Director, Frank, who told me to meet him at the downtown airport in BA the next morning.

Damn, I hope this isn't another ass chewing, like the last time we met there.

I hopped on the early AP flight to BA the next morning, and met with Frank at the in-town airport, still wondering what it was all about. I was even more curious when Frank said he would buy me breakfast in the lounge and that I would be returning to Asuncion on the next flight out.

What the hell was going on?

When we got our coffee and the waiter was out of ear shot I asked, "Frank, what is this all about? Have I screwed up like the last time we met here and you chewed my ass out?"

Frank thought this was funny and laughingly told me, "No, you didn't screw up. In fact, your office is the only one in the whole Region that always has their vouchers and expense accounts done correctly and in on time. We need you to do a job. We found out that Dick had not filled out an expense voucher for the whole year he was in Quito, not even for his move from the States. He just kept getting cash advances from the Embassy."

"Wow! How much did he get?"

Frank continued, "As close as we can figure over $11,000 and that doesn't include what he got for his move from Houston. So, I want you to go up there and reconstruct his vouchers. The secretary says he kept a lot of receipts but she doesn't know squat about anything."

Since things were quiet in Paraguay, I said, "OK, it might take a week or so."

"Take whatever time is necessary. Just get it done."

Since Quito sat in a bowl at 9000 feet surrounded by mountains, the commercial jets could only land there in the daylight and the trip would require an overnight in Lima, Peru, both coming and going.

After I cabled the US Embassy in Quito with my travel plans, they responded that someone would meet my flight.

As the Boeing 707 neared Quito I looked out the right window and saw we were flying parallel to a mountain ridge with a large ritzy hotel built on it. The pilot then banked sharply to the right, put down the landing gear and put on full flaps and started a steep descent.

Wow, this was getting exciting.

The pilot flared the plane out, hit the tarmac with tires screeching, powered the reverse thrusters and the plane came to a shuddering halt.

Well, we *have defied death and destruction one more time!*

We then taxied to the parking area where a set of stairs was rolled out to the front door of the aircraft and we all began to deplane.

As I walked towards the terminal, a tall, slender American with a pencil thin moustache stood there wearing dark trousers, a white dress shirt with a blue cravat, a plaid vest, blue blazer and leaning on a British style umbrella. If he had been wearing a bowler hat, he could have been Mr. Steed from the British TV series, *The Avengers*.

Sure enough, he came over to me, smiled and said, "Welcome to Quito, my name is Tom Smith, I'm with the consular office."

I shook his hand, saying, "Another Smith. There certainly are a bunch of you in the Foreign Service."

We retrieved my luggage and were on our way. As usual, there was the ubiquitous green GM carryall waiting for us outside the terminal. Our first stop was at the Hotel Americana, the second best hotel in Quito after the one I had seen on the mountain ridge as I was flying in.

The hotel was a massive three story concrete structure done in modern European style with all of the amenities you would expect from a four star hotel. After checking in, Tom and I rode the elevator to the third floor, and as we were walking down the hall to my room, I noticed a large nine inch wide rubber gasket around the entire hallway, encircling the floor, both walls and the ceiling.

"Tom, what the hell is this?"

Tom laughed, "The hotel is actually three separate buildings, the center with the elevators and the lobby, and the two wings with the guest rooms. You know Ecuador has more earthquakes than anywhere else in South America and large buildings have a way of cracking or collapsing during the tremors."

Well, I had just learned another interesting fact about Quito.

After emptying my suitcase, we left for the Embassy, again in the green carryall, which seems to be the standard official US Embassy transportation everywhere in the world or at least in Central and South America. The government must have gotten a good deal on them from General Motors.

At the Embassy, which was only four blocks up the hill, Tom introduced me to the US Marine Guard on duty; we then proceeded up the stairs to the second floor. It was laid out just as in Asuncion, only US employees permitted on the upper floors; the local employees being restricted to the first floor.

Tom led me to the Deputy Chief of Mission's, (DCM) office saying, "My office is just down the hall. I'll see you at quitting time. We can have a drink together."

"OK, can we try the fancy hotel on the top of the hill?"

"The Continental? Sure, they make a fantastic martini, the food is great and they have an excellent selection of Chilean reds. It's the best place in town." I noticed that Tom went to the Political office and not the consular office, which was on the first floor.

I introduced myself to the DCM's secretary, a thirty year old, five foot two blonde, dressed in an expensive black business suit with a sheer pale blue blouse covering a pair of 32Cs which were encased in a dark blue, low cut, lacy bra. She smiled and said, "Mr. Rayner, the DCM is expecting you. Please follow me."

She then rose and sashayed to the heavy inner office door, knocked, opened the door and announced, "Mr. Rayner to see you, sir."

I went through the door and met Mr. Olsen, a tall, slender man with steel rimmed glasses and graying short hair about forty five years old. He was dressed in a three piece Armani charcoal gray suit, long sleeved white monogrammed shirt and a regimental tie, your typical high- ranking Embassy officer attire. I must have looked a little scruffy next to him, wearing my standard travelling outfit with a blue blazer, open necked golf shirt, khaki trousers and my custom made black leather Argentine loafers.

Mr. Olsen rose from behind his desk, came around and warmly shook my hand, telling me what a fine man Dick was and what a tragic loss his death had been. He then stated that the Embassy staff was at my disposal and would help in any way possible.

I thanked him for his offer of assistance and said, "Well, I better go meet the BNDD secretary and get started."

His secretary then walked me down the hall and pointed out the

BNDD office smiling and saying, "If you need anything at all just give me a call, and I do mean anything."

I thanked her, turned and knocked on the office door, opened it and walked in. The secretary, sitting behind her desk, stood up and immediately burst into tears.

Oh shit, this is just what I need, another weeper and wailer.

I glanced at the name plate and said, "Anne. Please. There is nothing we can do to change the fact that Dick is dead."

Wrong again.

Anne's tears only got worse.

"Look, I'm going to the men's room, when I get back, I expect you to have gotten a grip on yourself and be ready to help me with this situation. Alright?"

I placed my attaché case on a chair, turned and left the office. Once outside, I said, "Hell, I don't even know where the men's room is."

Fortunately, another staff officer was coming down the corridor and pointed me in the right direction.

After using the facilities, I went down the stairs, through the front door and lit up a cigarette.

Man, this is NOT going to be easy!

What have I gotten myself into?

Oh well, I better get back upstairs and get started.

When I got back to the BNDD office, I was happy to see Anne had pulled herself together and was ready to start on the task at hand. As we both entered Dick's office Anne said, "I haven't touched a thing except to give Dick's wife his personal things."

"She didn't take his daily activity log or anything official, did she?"

"No. Only some family pictures and some personal stuff. What is a daily activity thingy, anyway?"

Great, how was I to put this puzzle together, if Dick's wife had carried off something that might give me a clue to the money trail, and he didn't keep a daily diary. This was getting worse by the minute!

I then sat down in the chair behind the desk and asked, "Where did he keep his travel records and stuff?"

Anne, with a look of triumph on her face, pulled open the large 8 by 12 file drawer on the right side of the desk, pointed and said, "There!"

She was right. The drawer was crammed full of receipts, invoices, bills and notes. Not in any order, just stuffed into the drawer. *Augggh!*

My first step in straightening out the mess was to read all of the case files and informant files that were in the office. Thank God, Dick had at least been diligent in writing up his operational activities.

By now, it was quitting time and I was looking forward to having a few drinks, dinner and a good night's sleep. Tomorrow, I would start digging into the labyrinth that faced me.

With perfect timing, Tom walked into the office and said, "You look like you could use a drink. Are you ready to go?"

I was more than ready and said, "Lead on!"

In the parking lot, Tom and I got into his personal car, a three year old Toyota, and without further ado, we drove up the winding road to the Hotel Continental. While he drove, Tom explained that the Continental was a five star hotel, and all of the rich people from Guayaquil summered there when the weather got unbearable in Guayaquil, which was located on the coast at the equator.

As we approached the gated front entrance, I saw the four story hotel was also built of heavy concrete in a modern style with the lobby in the center and two wings extending out along the ridgeline for the guest rooms, all of which had balconies overlooking the valleys on either side. There were two outdoor swimming pools, a set of lighted tennis courts, shuffle board and bocce courts and groupings of tables and chairs with large sun umbrellas, striped in the national color of Ecuador.

Tom evidently frequented the place, for, as we pulled up to the front portico the valet came rushing out, opened Tom's door and greeted him by name.

Tom gave his car keys to the valet and we walked up the steps to the massive front doors, which were opened by two bell hops, who also greeted Tom by name.

The reception area and lobby was three stories high. Modern art murals depicting the glories of the Inca Nation covered the walls from the floor up to the vaulted dome ceiling. There were huge glass windows on the rear overlooking the wide valley that stretched for miles before ending in the next high range of the Andes. It was more impressive than anything I had ever seen and put the vistas of our Grand Canyon to shame.

Off to the right rear of the lobby was a modern, well stocked bar with a dozen groupings of plush red leather chairs set around shiny onyx coffee tables, all focused on the fantastic view out the rear windows.

A young waitress, dressed in tight black pants, a white blouse and a black vest quickly appeared and took our drink orders.

Tom said, "My usual, Maria."

I ordered, "A double Beefeaters on the rocks, hold the vermouth and with a large olive, please."

In no time our waitress reappeared with two icy cocktail shakers and two glasses into which she poured our drinks. She set the cocktail shakers on the table and said in excellent English, "Call me when you're ready for another."

This is just what I needed after my day in Hell.

After two drinks, we entered the dining room which was done in deep red velvet drapes, crystal glass lighting fixtures and tables covered in white damask, set with full bone china place settings with a gold crest of arms on them and the appropriate heavy silverware.

On the maitre de's suggestion I ordered the veal scaloppini with a small salad. Tom grabbed the wine list and ordered a bottle of premium Chilean Concha y Toro Cabernet to go with our meals. The meal was outstanding, but it was getting late and I had a full day at the office the next day so we passed on the elegant postre tray.

We left the Hotel Continental and Tom drove back to the Americana. It had been an exhausting day and I was ready for a cold shower and a good night's sleep.

When I got to my room, the sheets were turned down and the complimentary Godiva chocolate was on my pillow. After my shower I hit the bed and as usual, I placed my S&W Model 39 automatic on the bed stand before dropping off to sleep.

At about 3:30 AM, I awoke with a start. Someone was rattling on my door, trying to break in. I sat up, grabbed my gun and started to stand up. When I got to my feet I realized the floor was shaking. It was an earthquake! I sat back down on the bed, lit up a cigarette and thought *by the time I throw on my clothes and make it down the hall and out to the stairs, the building will have collapsed. So I might as well go back to sleep.*

Welcome to Quito Gordon, you're getting the whole enchilada.

The next morning, after an excellent American style breakfast, fresh squeezed orange juice, a couple of soft scrambled eggs with a rasher of bacon and American style toast and a pot of rich hot Ecuadorean coffee, I was ready to face the day.

I left the hotel and slowly walked to the Embassy. It was about sixty degrees, the sky a brilliant blue and clear of any pollution, the sun was shining and the birds were singing. Today was definitely going to be better than yesterday.

Entering the office, I saw Anne was already behind her desk. She quickly apologized for her actions of the previous day, saying she and her husband had been close friends with Dick and his wife and she had been reminiscing about the good times they had had together. She promised she would do better now that she had gotten it out of her system.

I replied, "I know what you are going through. So, let's get started. The first thing I want you to do is open the file drawers, while I go down to the Admin Office and find out exactly how much money Dick had drawn out. I want to read all the operational and administrative reports to get a feel for how Dick's operation was going here.

I proceeded down to the Admin office and obtained copies of Dick's vouchers for the Official Advance Fund which totaled $11,500. Fortunately, I discovered Dick's housing and utilities had been paid directly by the Embassy meaning that I didn't have to worry about those expenditures.

By the time I returned to the office, Anne had pulled all of the files and had them stacked on my desk. I poured myself a cup of the great local coffee and told Anne, "This is going to take a lot of concentration. Please hold all the calls and see that I am not disturbed. Oh, see if you can get me the RD in Buenos Aires on the phone."

Five minutes later I was on the phone with Frank, explaining how big the problem was and that it would take much longer than either of us had envisioned. His only response was to do what was necessary.

I started reviewing the files and to my surprise found a copy of Dick's funds withdrawal from the Houston office immediately before he was transferred. This gave me a date to start with, as well as a total amount, $16,500, I had to reconcile. This was the first good news I had.

I continued reading the administrative files, and by lunch time, I had a rough outline of Dick's activities for the year he was in Quito. There were several gaps, but at least I had an idea how to proceed.

When I started to leave for lunch, Anne said, "Richard Kirkendal, the US Customs Attaché, stopped by and wants to meet you."

"Great, where is his office? Maybe we can catch lunch together."

"Second door to the left."

I walked down the hall and knocked on his door. Shortly, Rich opened the door and said, "Come on in. You must be Rayner."

"That's me. Glad to meet you. Are you related to Carl Kirkendal, a Narc in McAllen, Texas? You like just like him."

Rich laughed, "Yeah, that's my older brother. How you know him?"

"Oh, a few years ago when I was in New Orleans, I ran a U/C deal down in McAllen for 10,000 Black Beauties and Carl was my backup. I thought he said he had a brother in Customs, but he didn't say where."

"Yeah, I was stationed in El Paso and came down here about the same time Dick did. Too bad what happened in Curacao. Dick and I worked together a lot and I wanted to cover him on the deal in Curacao, but Washington wouldn't let me go. Said it wasn't Customs' job. Piece of shit isn't it."

"From what I hear, he really could have used a trained Agent to back him, BNDD or Customs, doesn't matter. Hell, even a CIA agent would have been better than trying to do it solo with only untrained locals for support."

Rich shrugged, "You ready for some lunch?"

"Sure, how's the food in the Embassy cafeteria?"

"Not bad if you only want a sandwich or something light. But, if you want a big meal we'll have to go out."

"Nah, a sandwich would be just fine. I went up to the Continental with Tom, the spook, last night."

"Ha, been there and done that. We'll grab a sandwich downstairs."

As we were walking down the stairs, Rich apologized for not meeting me when I arrived, saying, "I was out for two days in the weeds with the Feds trying to find some opium patches, but we didn't have any luck. Just did a lot of walking in the sun."

The cafeteria was one of the better ones I had eaten in while in South America. Though small, it would have fit in anywhere in the US, with the standard choices of American food, cheeseburgers, BLTs, French fries, and tuna fish salad on toast, which I opted for with an iced tea. Dick chose the BLT and we settled for a small table in a corner where not everybody would overhear us.

Rich said, "I know about Dick's laziness when it came to doing administrative work. He just couldn't bring himself to do it. I knew it would catch up with him sooner or later. It's too bad it had to be like this."

"Yeah, I'm having a hard time even telling when he was in town or travelling or what."

"Oh, I can help you with that. We used to back each other up and did most things together."

"Really? Do you have your reports and travel vouchers for those times?"

"Hey, I told you Dick had the problem with the paper work, not me."

"Man, Rich, if you could let me see your stuff, it'll save me from having to creatively reconstruct some of his travels and expenses. You are a prince."

"When do you want to start?"

I said, "Give me a couple of days to get a feel for it. I'll be in touch. And, I'm buying the drinks and dinner tonight, only not at the Continental, I don't know if my system or my wallet can stand that. Maybe I can make you an informant and cover the cost of dinner that way."

"Now that is creative financing! You've got yourself a deal."

I decided the first order of business was to reconstruct Dick's move from Houston to Quito. I had found out from the embassy Admin officer that Dick and his family had spent a week at the Americana Hotel before moving into their permanent quarters, so they would have eaten all their meals at restaurants, had their dry cleaning and laundry done and paid for the gas for the car the Embassy had given them. I obtained a menu from the hotel and calculated three meals a day for Dick, his wife and two children. I assumed they hadn't skimped on the meals and had left gracious tips to the wait staff and other hotel employees. That took care of the first $2,000. I was on my way.

I took my notes and walked out to Anne's office, "Prepare this first travel voucher on Dick's move."

Anne said, "I've never done a travel voucher before. What do they look like?"

I said, "Forget it; I'll have my secretary In Asuncion do it next week when I go back." I guess I couldn't blame Anne too much as she was the wife of an embassy employee and had been hired locally with no idea how BNDD operated.

Remembering I had paid taxes and fees when my car and personal household possessions had arrived in Paraguay, I added some of these costs and knocked off another $1000.

Next, I started separating all of the receipts chronologically by month and found there were receipts from Mexico City and Buenos Aires in with the ones from Ecuador. What was this?

Then I remembered that I had met Dick at the interagency conference in Mexico City the previous year and at a Regional meeting in Buenos Aires in January. Now, when I get back to Asuncion, I can pull out my vouchers and copy my expenses onto Dick's travel voucher. Fortunately, I didn't have to worry about the cost of the airplane fares, as we all used Government Travel Requests (GTR) and booked our travel through the Embassy's travel office when travelling internationally.

By the time I had gotten the receipts into order, I realized I had spent ten days in Quito and was ready to take a little R&R, go home to

Asuncion, get reacquainted with my family and tend to business at my own office.

The next day, I hopped the Braniff flight to Lima, Peru, spent the night and took the Braniff flight to Asuncion.

I spent the next week catching up on the work in my office that had accumulated and I had my secretary, Donnie, fill out the travel vouchers for Dick's transfer to Quito, the trip to Mexico City and the regional conference in Buenos Aires and sent them via the diplomatic pouch to the regional office.

The next Monday I flew back to Lima, again spent the night and arrived in Quito the following afternoon. I knew what I had already accomplished was the easy part of the task. Undercover travel could not be booked through the embassy travel office with a GTR, but had to be paid in cash. It would have been stupid to pay for your ticket with a GTR and then have the violator you were meeting with read your ticket and discover that it was paid for by the US government. It could have been fatal.

I threw myself into the task at hand. First, I read all of Dick's operational reports, compared them to Rich's reports and started correlating the receipts with their itineraries. I spent several evenings with Rich, picking his brain and jogging his memory. "If you met these two bad guys in a bar, how many drinks did you buy?"

"Did Dick pay for them?"

"Did Dick leave a big tip?"

"How much did the taxi cost and who paid for it?"

"When you met the bad guys at a restaurant did Dick pay for the meals and drinks?"

Finally, Rich cried out, "Christ, you're as bad as Internal Affairs! I can't remember every detail, I was more interested in making sure nobody blew our cover or pulled guns on us."

By Friday afternoon, my mind was whirling. I told Rich, "Enough of this greasy carryout Chinese food and warm Cokes. If I see another egg roll I'm going to puke. Let's go the Continental, have a few cold martinis and talk about other stuff!"

Rich heartily agreed and we were off to the Continental.

When out drinks arrived, I saluted Rich with my glass and said, "It must be five o'clock somewhere."

"Salud."

I responded, "y pesetas y amor. Y tiempo para gastarles." 'Health, money and love, and time to enjoy them.'

It was a relaxing enjoyable evening. We discussed the upcoming merger between BNDD and the Customs agents working on narcotics and the ramifications it would have. We talked about mutual acquaintances, where we had been stationed and about how we had gotten started in Federal law enforcement. Surprisingly, both of us had started out chasing wetbacks in the Border Patrol on the southern border, which led to more reminiscing about mutual friends in the Patrol, many of whom had later transferred to either Customs or BNDD.

Saturday morning I slept in and, not wanting to go back to the office, I spent the day walking the streets and markets of Quito like a tourist. What a great way to recharge my batteries.

By 10 o'clock Sunday morning I was back at the office putting more pieces of the puzzle together and by Tuesday afternoon had gotten to the point that I thought it was time to let Anne try her hand at creating Dick's travel vouchers. I had brought copies of some of my old travel vouchers with me and handed them to Anne, saying, "It's time for you to learn how to do these. I'm going back to Asuncion tomorrow so you will have a week to play with them. See what you can do."

There were still some spaces in Dick's calendar and some receipts left, but I would work on them on my next trip.

My first morning back in Asuncion I called Frank in Buenos Aires and reported where I was in the task and asked him if he could find out what investigation Dick was working on, who the case Agent was and could I find out the time line for Dick's trip to Curacao. Frank said he would get on it and have the information pouched to the Quito office by the time I returned there the following week.

By the following weekend, I made my way back to Quito and as excepted there was the information I had requested from Frank. During my absence Anne had finished the vouchers I had left with her and seemed to be confident about doing travel vouchers.

I found Dick had travelled to Miami, spent two days there and then flew to Curacao with the informant to have initial discussions with the violator. The Miami office decided that since this was just a preliminary meeting, it was not necessary to have backup Agents accompany Dick and the informant.

I now had enough information to put together a hypothetical voucher with the expenditures Dick would have had. It was good enough for me. Within two days I had completed the outline and set Anne to work on typing this voucher. I added up all of Dick's expenditures I had documented and found that I had less than $1,000 outstanding. Then it hit me. Dick must have met with some of his informants in Quito and paid them some funds. So, back through the

Informant files I went, noting the meetings Dick had with Informants in Quito and there in a separate envelope were the receipts for the payments he had made. Hooray, at least I didn't have to create these from my head.

Adding the costs of some meals and drinks with the Informants, I totaled up numbers. The government owed Dick $350.00!

Two days later, with the outstanding vouchers in hand, I bid fond farewell to Quito and flew home to Asuncion. Two days later I proudly walked into Frank's office in Buenos Aires, placed the vouchers on his desk and stated, "Mission accomplished!!"

Chapter 24

No Good Deed Goes Unpunished

It was now getting to be the summer of 1973, and one morning I was sitting in my office, with my feet on the desk thinking about the future. I had three months to go on my two year tour of duty in Paraguay.

If I signed up for another two or three year tour, the family and I could get thirty days free home leave (the government paying our travel expenses) and with time for consultations at headquarters, a total of forty five days back in the states without using any of my annual leave. Not a bad deal and with money we were saving due to our housing, utilities and domestic help being paid for by the government, we were living in high cotton and could get healthy financially.

In walked my secretary who said, "The Marine guard just called and said the money changer is downstairs and very excited and needs to talk to you right away."

"Okay. Donnie, go down and get him and bring him up. God, I hope it's not another one of those screwy deals like the last one in Bolivia."

Nothing like going undercover in Santa Cruz, Bolivia with no backup, and running into the DCM and Political Officer on vacation with their wives in the hotel where I was going to meet the bad guys. Christ, Commandante Guido didn't even trust his own Feds stationed in Santa Cruz.

"Hola, Cambio, how are you this fine morning? Have any good exchange rates?"

"Oh, Senor Rayner, you always make the joke. No, this is very serious. The police just picked up El Gordo."

"What for? I was talking to Campos Alum the other day, and everything seemed fine."

"The problem is that the Spanish version of the Reader's Digest arrived here yesterday, and it has the story of Senor Ricord in it. I guess they think El Gordo had something to do with it."

"Oh, Shit! Carlos, come in here; we have a big problem."

Carlos entered the office, came to attention with an exaggerated salute and said, "Oui mon general."

"Knock it off. Cambio here has some bad news, and I want him to repeat it to you, just to make sure I didn't misunderstand him."

Cambio repeated what he had told me, "El Gordo and I were to have coffee at the Plaza, like we usually do. Instead, El Gordo's wife shows up and tells me the police came to their house last evening and arrested El Gordo. She asked the police what he was being arrested for and they said crimes against the State."

"Crimes against the State! What the hell is that?" Carlos gasped.

Cambio looked at Carlos, smiled and said, "Anything they want it to be."

"Oh, crap, Donnie, call the DCM and tell him I have to talk to him, the Political Officer and the Chief of Station (CIA) sometime today. We have a slight problem."

"Carlos, you get a full debrief from Cambio, give him some money, and tell him to keep in touch. We have to find out what the hell is going on."

Carlos and Cambio went into the other office, and I walked downstairs to the Consul's Office to meet with G. Garrett, whose secretary said he was in the cafeteria.

I walked into the cafeteria and spotted G. Garrett sitting alone at a table in a well-tailored Seville Row three-piece dark brown wool suit, vest completely buttoned, a monogrammed white shirt with tiger eye cuff links, and the standard imperial red State Department power tie expertly done in a Windsor knot. As usual, he was wearing highly polished cordovan wingtips with matching OTC stockings. He could have just stepped out of the latest issue of *Esquire* or *GQ*. G. Garrett was reading "El Diario," the local newspaper, holding the paper away from his clothing as if to insure none of the ink rubbed onto him.

As I grabbed a cup of café doble, I mused, *well, they won't have any difficulty telling us apart. But, at least my chinos are clean and have a crease in them and my golf shirt isn't striped or plaid.*

I walked over to G. Garrett's table, pulled out a chair, smiled, and said, "You better put your cloak and dagger back on. We have a slight problem."

What little color there was in his face drained as if the plug had been pulled, and he rasped, "What did you do now?"

"Me? I didn't do anything, but the local Reader's Digest came out yesterday with the Ricord story in it. Plus, they arrested El Gordo last night. They must be pretty pissed."

"What does that have to do with me?"

"Well, you and I know that El Gordo didn't have anything to do with this but if they squeeze his nuts real hard, he may try to give up anybody he can. I don't even think he knows your man, but with what's going down, you might want to drop a dime on your source and give him a heads up."

"Geez, I knew this was going to be a problem. I should have never gotten involved with this secret spy shit."

"Ah, come on G. Garrett, you know you had fun doing this and with the letter I wrote to State about your outstanding work on this case, you'll probably get a raise or something."

"Screw you Rayner!"

"Well, I just thought I'd keep you up to date on everything. Oh, by the way, I'm setting up a meeting with the DCM, the Politico, and the Agency this afternoon on this. Do you want to join us?"

"No, no, no. Keep me out of it."

"Okay, I won't say anything about it. See you later. And hey, I like your suit. It makes you look very diplomatic."

"Like I said. Screw you Rayner."

When I got back to my office, I found that Carlos and Cambio were gone.

"Donnie, where the hell are they? I told Carlos to take Cambio's statement so I could document everything."

"Relax Mr. Rayner, Carlos found out that Cambio is also an old friend of El Gordo's connection with the Policia. You know the Sergeant Major."

I nodded.

She continued, "So they went out to see him and find out what they can. Oh, your meeting with the DCM, et al, is set for 2:00 PM."

By the time two o'clock rolled around, there was still no word from Carlos.

Because I could not verify the account of what really happened to El Gordo, I was going to have a hard time convincing this overly cautious diplomatic group, but I knew Cambio had been telling me the truth about the Feds snatching up El Gordo. So into the meeting I went.

All of those present were surprised at what had happened and started justifying the arrest on other grounds, like maybe El Gordo was a thief, or a bank robber, or had killed someone, or raped a woman, or was a subversive, or whatever, not just for cooperating with BNDD. They gave my information a 30% credibility rating.

It was finally agreed, that the Chief of Station would meet with Campos Alum, the deputy attorney general, a CIA source, and find out what the truth was. In the mean time, BNDD would continue their investigation and we would all have a meeting the following day in the Ambassador's office.

At about 6:30 that evening, Carlos pulled up at my house and said he had some news about El Gordo.

"Come on in, Carlos. You sure look like you need a drink."

"Thanks, Gordon. I certainly could use one."

Once he was in my living room, I told Ella Mae, "Ask Vicky to bring us the orange juice, some ice and the bottle of Stolis that's in the freezer and a couple of glasses. This looks like it is going to be a long session with Harvey Wallbanger."

After Vicky had brought in the drink fixings and returned to the kitchen, I started making the drinks and Carlos nervously motioned to me, "Don't waste the juice in the first one. I'll take the Stolis neat."

Man, something must have really gotten to Carlitos; I know he did some heavy undercover work in New York and he is a solid street agent and I have never seen him toss down liquor straight.

"Easy, Carlitos, relax. Hey, I bet you didn't even have lunch today. I'll have Vicky feed the kids now and then we can have dinner together after a few Bangers and without any distractions."

Carlos finally calmed down and related his experiences of the afternoon.

"Cambio convinced me the easiest way to get information was for us to just drive down to police headquarters and ask the Sgt-Major what was happening."

I gasped in alarm, "This isn't for real! You just can't do things like that in this country. Shit, they could have locked both of you up and made you disappear permanently. Then what would I do? No partner, no G-car, no informants. Do you realize how many reports I'd have to write?"

Well, this broke the tensions. Carlos laughed nervously, "Yeah, but I have my diplomatic status. They wouldn't do anything like that? Would they?"

"My boy let us not push our luck too far. Anyway what happened?"

"You wouldn't believe it. We parked right out in front of the headquarters building, marched up to the gate, where I flashed my badge to the guard, identified myself as the Attaché from the US Embassy and demanded to see the Sgt-Major. Believe it or not, after five minutes, they let us in and showed us down the hallway to his office waiting room, where a detective told us to sit down and the Sgt.-Major would see us in a few minutes."

"I can't believe it Carlos."

"Well, things went south from there. The Sgt.-Major didn't show up. We waited most of the afternoon and when we went to leave we discovered the door to the waiting room was locked and we were stuck inside. They had us there for over two hours."

"This sounds like the Keystone Cops. Carlos, what happened then?"

"This isn't funny Gordon! Anyway, after beating on the door for several minutes, a different cop unlocked the door and profusely apologized, saying the Sgt.-Major had been in a meeting all day and couldn't see us until tomorrow. He didn't know why the first guy left us in the room and nobody knew anything. He said for us to come back in the morning."

Carlos stopped to take a breath and I asked, "Okay, so what are your plans? The Station Chief, Phil Ernst, is going to meet with Campos Alum early in the morning and later, all of us heavies are going to have another meeting with the Ambassador when he gets back. So, see what you and Cambio can do"

"Cambio thinks we can get in to see the Sgt.-Major tomorrow morning if we get down to his office early."

"Okay, do what you can. If we can't get any confirmation, we are shit out of luck. I think Campos Alum is going to stonewall us on the whole deal. I just hope they don't make El Gordo disappear."

"Yeah, me too. Let me get out of here, Gordon, I have to meet Cambio at early thirty so I need to get some rest. I'll see you as soon as I can tomorrow."

"Goodnight Carlitos, take care of yourself."

The next morning, I arrived at the Embassy in time to stand at attention and watch the Marine Guard raise the American flag at 0800 hours like they do every day at every Marine post around the globe. It made me proud every time I saw the ceremony. Well at least the day was starting out well.

At about 9:05, as I was reviewing the overnight cable traffic, the DCM walked into my office, motioned for the secretary to leave, closed the outer and inner office doors and sat down across from me at my desk. *This is serious stuff! He is the number two man in the embassy and usually he would call me into his office when he wanted to talk. Oh, Oh.*

"Gordon, this is an important matter and I don't think you fully realize what is happening. You see the Ambassador has advised Washington that the Paraguayan government is fully cooperating in the Ricord matter as well as every narcotic enforcement endeavor. If you continue to raise a stink about this alleged arrest of your informant for talking to Readers Digest it will reflect poorly not only on the Ambassador, but on the whole staff here in Asuncion."

"Well, I certainly wouldn't want anything like that to happen. You know El Gordo had nothing to do with the Readers Digest Interview, but sir, they grabbed his ass just because he's my informant and God knows what they are doing to him. I can't just turn a blind eye to what is going on. Damn, I owe the man something. Don't I?"

"I'm sorry, Gordon, that's the way it is. Sometimes you have to accept a little collateral damage for the greater good. You do what you have to do. Just don't make it a big issue. You know what I mean?"

"Yes sir. Thank you for telling me how the game is played. I thought we all dealt in facts, but then I don't have much training in the bull shit part of foreign affairs."

"Yes, we have discussed your naivety several times at our staff meetings."

"Oh, I thought I was one of the staff."

"Ha. No, Gordon you are just an attached agency that we have to put up with. Anyway, we'll see you when the Station Chief gets back. Remember what I told you."

After the DCM had left my office, I sat there stunned. *This couldn't be happening. I am hardly a bleeding heart liberal when it comes to civil rights and what have you, but you just can't let someone hang out there to swing in the wind due to political bullshit.*

At about 10:15 I got a call that Ernst, the chief of station had returned and we were set for the meeting at 10:30 in the Ambassador's office. Well, at least today I had worn my three piece charcoal suit, white shirt with gold cuff links and my own version of a power tie, which was actually a regimental stripe in USMC scarlet and gold which I purchased at a Marine Corps PX. *Time to go into the lion's den!!*

As I entered the Ambassador's conference room promptly at 10:25, I felt as if I had been set up for the slaughter like the proverbial sacrificial lamb. All of the section heads of the embassy, as well as the Military Attaché, the Colonel in charge of the MAG (Military Assistance Group) and G. Garrett, the US Consul were in attendance and already seated at the table, with only one seat left open for me at the far end of the table from the Ambassador.

Without much ado, the DCM summarized the situation and the CIA Chief of Station, Phil Ernst, related his conversation with Campos Alum, the 1st Deputy Attorney General of Paraguay. Ernst stated that Campos Alum at first denied any knowledge of El Gordo but then admitted he was in custody on a local political matter that did not relate to his working for BNDD or that was of any interest to the

United States.

The Ambassador cried out, "See, I told you this was being overblown and Rayner is just stirring up shit!"

Everyone nodded in agreement, like puppets on a string, except for the Mil Group commander, who just shook his head and winked at me. No questions to Ernst, no further explanation, just his statement on what Campos Alum had said.

My ship was sinking!

Then, as if I had given a signal, a secretary knocked on the door and said Agent Rivera had arrived and urgently wanted to see me. I told the group Carlos had been out with another source and had been to see the Sgt.-Major of the National Police about the incident and maybe they all would want to listen to the information he had gotten.

Carlos, a Puerto Rican who spoke English with a heavy accent, like a second language, entered the conference room and stopped dead in his tracks when he saw the assembled crowd.

Oh shit, Carlitos. Don't freeze up now!

I looked at the Ambassador. The Ambassador looked at me, Carlos, the DCM and Ernst and finally softly said, "Go ahead, Agent Rivera, tell us what you found out."

Carlos tried to speak but started stuttering. I said, "Carlos, if it would be easier to tell us in Spanish, go ahead. All of us here can understand." And even the Ambassador nodded in agreement.

Carlos smiled, relaxed and then proceeded to relate what he and Cambio had found out that morning. He said they had gone to the Police Headquarters at 6:30 to wait for the Sgt.-Major, who was scheduled to come to work at 7 AM, the usual start of the Paraguayan business day. Sure enough, they saw the Sgt.-Major walking towards the front door at about ten minutes before seven. So they got out of the car and approached him.

Carlos continued. Cambio then greeted the Sgt.-Major in Guaraní, the local Indian language and introduced Carlos to him. Carlos stated that the Sgt.-Major wasn't the least bit upset, and when Cambio told him they were interested in what had happened to El Gordo, another friend of the Sgt.-Major's, He said, "Oh, sure. Come on into my office and we will find out if anything has happened to him over night since I last saw him."

When they got to his office and had been served coffee, the Sgt.-Major told an officer to go and find out what the status of El Gordo was. While they waited, Carlos asked, "Why was El Gordo arrested?"

"Oh, the usual political stuff. General Martinez, the Commander in Chief of the Army, called the Attorney General to tell him how upset he was with the Readers Digest article and he wanted the source of the information to be found and *interrogated*. Well, you know, shit flows down hill and I finally was told to go pick up El Gordo and bring him in for questioning."

"Who told you to do this?"

"Oh, somebody in the Attorney General's office. I didn't take the call myself, but my assistant indicated it came from 'the top'. And yes, they did mention El Gordo by name. So I had my officers pick him up the other night."

"Was this unusual?" Carlos asked.

"Not really, we pick people up all the time. Usually for political reasons, you know, like writing an editorial for that damn communist newspaper, "El Rosado."

The assistant came back into the office and handed a piece of paper to the Sgt.-Major, who casually read it, dropped it on the desk and said, "Well, El Gordo is okay."

Cambio asked, "Can I pay for him to have some breakfast? You know from where you get yours."

The Sgt.-Major laughed, patting his rotund stomach "Oh sure, I forgot you're familiar with the food in here. As you can see, I don't eat this slop."

"What happens to him now?" asked Carlos. "Well, we will just hold him until we get word from the Attorney General's Office. We asked him everything about the Reader's Digest thing, but I'm sure he doesn't know anything about it and I told the AG that."

"Oh?"

"Hey, Cambio, tell this gringo about our interrogation techniques."

Cambio nodded and said, "Oh yes, Carlos, if El Gordo knows anything about the Reader's Digest thing he would have told the Sgt.-Major. They are very effective in their questioning."

"Okay, Sgt.-Major, thank you very much for your efforts. Here's a little something for your flower fund."

"Why thank you senor. Any time we can be of service, let me know."

After relating the above conversation to the group, Carlos looked at me and said, "That's all there is. Are there any questions?"

The silence was deafening. So, I thanked Carlos and told him to go to our office and I would see him later.

After Carlos left, I glanced down the table at the Ambassador, who looked like he was going to go ballistic. After a full minute of silence he had calmed down and quietly said, "Well, it appears we have conflicting views on what actually has taken place. I tend to give Mr. Ernst's version more credibility than some enlisted police officer's wild story of what happened."

"That's right, Sir, I don't think we should jump to any rash conclusions about this," whined the Political Officer as a chorus of heads around the table bobbed in unison. "We have to be very careful in what we do."

The Ambassador rose and said, "Thank you all for coming, gentlemen. If there is anything else we need to discuss. I will advise you." This ended our meeting.

As I was slowly walking back to my office, the Mil Group Colonel came up behind me and whispered, "You really stuck it to them this time, Gordon. But watch your back! This isn't over yet by a long shot, so covers your ass."

"Thanks Colonel, I'm glad to hear the world isn't completely mad. Don't worry; I'll take care of myself."

Carlos and I then went down to the cafeteria to talk and get our shit together on what had happened and what we were going to do. As we were mulling over our plans, my secretary came in and told me the DCM wanted to see me ASAP. So I told Carlos, "Come on, let's go see what they want this time."

"Ah, Mr. Rayner, I think the DCM wants to see you one on one and not with Agent Rivera."

"Okay, no witnesses, this is going to be interesting."

Two minutes later the DCM's secretary showed me into office and closed the door behind me. I turned and said, "Yes Sir, you wanted to see me?"

"Yes, Agent Rayner, the Ambassador seems to think you are not entirely on board with his decision on this matter, so he has instructed me to advise you that from now on your authority to sign off on cables or any reports is rescinded and you will get everything approved by me or the Political Officer before it is sent out."

I was speechless. "I have never heard of anything like this, sir. As an independent agency, I thought I had the authority to run my own shop with only consultations and guidelines from you all."

"Well, usually that is true but these are unusual times that call for unusual actions."

"I see. Does this mean you want to see all of my admin reports and time cards and stuff like that?"

"To start with. Yes, everything. We will see how it works out."

"Thank you. I guess I have to go back to my office and write up something on this."

"Mr. Rayner, don't be a smart ass. Do just what I said to do. The Ambassador was so pissed that he was going to have you declared Persona No Grata and have you out of the country in 48 hours. I convinced him that since you only have three more months to do on your tour of duty, it would be less of a problem to just do it this way."

"Yes sir. Thank you, I guess."

The rest of the day was an almost complete blur. I was caught between a rock and a hard spot. I was technically a member of the country team at the embassy, but I was also a career Federal Narcotic Agent with the Department of Justice. The most the Ambassador or State Department could do was insure that I never served overseas again, but BNDD and Justice could screw up my whole career. I could end up in the Compliance Group in NYC or LA counting drugs in some cruddy pill mill.

Knowing my continued 'foreign service' career was in the crapper, I made up my mind to stand by my ethical beliefs and go around the Ambassador's orders and notify BNDD headquarters what was going on.

Carlos and I spent that evening and the next morning making handwritten notes on what had transpired. I was careful to stick to the factual evidence and not let my feelings enter into the material. Let someone else judge the whole situation.

The plan was for Carlos to take his handwritten notes to Regional Headquarters, relate to the regional director what had occurred and to prepare the Report of Investigation (ROI) for the case files in Buenos Aires and BNDD Hdq.

We had finished our work and had made Carlos' flight reservations to Buenos Aires for the next morning, when I got a call from the Marine Guard that El Gordo was in the lobby.

I was relieved and excited. "Wow, El Gordo is down stairs. Carlos, go down and bring him up to the office where we can both debrief him here in the office and no one will be the wiser."

El Gordo related, "I was at home and two police officers, who I knew, came to my door and said they had to take me in for questioning. I asked them what the charges are. The lead officer said, "Oh, you know. It's about that August Ricord thing."

I told them, "I didn't know anything about Ricord."

"Sorry, it doesn't matter. You know we're just doing our jobs."

El Gordo went on to say that when they got to the police station they took him to an interrogation room, stripped his clothes off, chained him to a chair and began to work him over.

"Did they use clubs to hit you?" I asked.

"No, Senor Rayner, they only used rolled up magazines and only hit me in the body, never in the face or head where I would bleed. After a few minutes, I told them that I would tell them everything about anything they wanted to know."

"The first thing they wanted to know was what I had been doing for you. Since I have never given you any information about the politicos, I told them everything we had done together, here, and in Bolivia."

"Well, that's good. It wasn't like we have done anything to upset them. Hell, nothing covert, that they didn't know about."

"Si, senor. That is what I figured. Then they started asking me about the Ricord thing and that's when they got mad because I couldn't tell them anything. After they beat me some more, I finally asked them what they wanted to know. They said the truth and where did I get the information I gave to that reporter. By this time I was crying and when I denied knowing anything, they said they would have to hurt me."

"Jesus, El Gordo, what did they think they had been doing to you at the time? How long did this go on?"

"Oh, I guess it was several hours. But, then my friend, the sub official, told me they were going to drown me. He apologized and said he knew I was telling the truth, but that's how it was done."

"Drown you. What did they do?"

"Well, I was still strapped in the chair, so they grabbed my hair, yanked my head back, threw a towel over my face and poured a bucket of water over my head. This continued until I fainted, I thought I had drowned. When I woke up they again asked me about Ricord. Damned, Senor Rayner, I wish I had known something to tell them, but I didn't, so they did it to me again. When I woke up the second time, I cried and cried, I guess they finally believed me, for they stopped for a while."

"What happened then?"

"Well, the next day they came in, fed me and said they were done, but were waiting for word on what to do with me. Then a few hours ago, they said I was free to leave and I left and went home to see my wife and change clothes and then I came here."

Since I was still under the Ambassador's embargo on sending out any cable traffic without approval, I told Carlos to take all of our notes and proceed to Buenos Aires the following day and write his reports from there. I then prepared a cable to Buenos Aires and Hdq outlining El Gordo's story and gave Carlos a carbon copy to carry to BA. I then went to the DCM and advised him of what had transpired and gave him my proposed cable for approval.

The DCM read the cable, looked at me and said, "We will discuss this cable with the Political officer and the Chief of Station, Ernst, and get back to you."

Two hours later the DCM called me into his office and handed me a copy of the cable he had approved and had sent. I looked at it and had a difficult time relating it to what I had given the DCM two hours previously. Instead of my language describing <u>Arrest, Interrogation and Torture there were phrases of Detained, Questioned on Political Matters and Released Unharmed.</u>

Chapter 25

Jack is Back

About a year and a half later, my tour in Asuncion was coming to a close. This Friday morning I was sitting in my office busy on administrative chores, when my secretary, Donnie, who was eight months pregnant, stepped into my office, holding her bulging stomach with a frightful look in her eyes. I thought, "Shit, she's going into labor!" I jumped up and said, "Donnie, are you all right?"

She gasped and said, "Jack is back!"

While working in the Embassy, I kept my S&W Model 39 pistol in a holster with a safety strap in my desk drawer so as not to upset the Embassy staff. My thoughts flashed back to my friend, Octavio Gonzales, who was the Agent in Charge in Bogota, Columbia, and had been killed when an informant walked into his office and shot him. Before I could react, Jack walked into my office, luckily unarmed, and demanded I turn over his pistol which he had left in the safe when he had been sent back to the States.

I professed ignorance of this and Jack said "That's all right; I'll get another one in Brazil."

I asked Jack, "How the hell did you get back into Paraguay?"

He laughed and said, "When they took away my diplomatic passport they let me keep the outside cover and I just put it over my tourist passport." He then turned and ran out of my office, down the stairs and out the front door of the Embassy.

My first thoughts were for my secretary, so I sat her at her desk and ran down the hall to the Communications Office, beat on the door, and told her husband, "Donnie needs you." I then ran to the other end of the hall to tell the Ambassador about Jack, but the Embassy was already on lock down; his office, as well as the other 2nd floor offices, was secured. I then called the US Marine Guard at Post 1, the front entrance to the Embassy, and determined that Jack was last seen running out the front gate of the grounds.

When things finally settled down, I called the Ambassador and advised him everything was secure and Jack was off the premises. He loudly screamed into the phone, "Get in here right now."

Shortly, there was a meeting with the Ambassador, the Charge', the chief political officer, the CIA station chief and myself. I tried to explain what had happened, but the Ambassador said, " I'm holding DEA and you responsible for Jack's appearance today and if Jack is not out of the country in 24 hours I'll declare the whole DEA Office 'persona non grata' and throw all of you out of Paraguay.

I returned to my office and called Frank, the Regional Director in Buenos Aires and told him what had occurred. His only response was "Do whatever you have to but, get it done, and I will back up whatever you do. Oh, try not to kill him."

I then met with Dave Jones and Carlos, my new agent, and told them what Jack has said. So, we decided Carlos would get with the locals and search the city while Dave and I checked out the hotels. I had no idea what we were going to do with Jack once we found him, but, one thing was sure, we were going to get him.

After checking most of the hotels, we learned the buses for Brazil left from the front of the Hotel Iguazu, the triangular hotel in downtown Asuncion. This hotel was a tourist favorite.

Dave and I walked into the Iguazu lobby at about 8:00 PM. The place was crowded with tourists, including a group of about 25 Americans, who were on a tour going to the Falls de Iguazu on the Parana River, which was the border between Paraguay and Brazil. Dave and I scanned the lobby. There was Jack, chatting with a couple of blue haired old ladies from Kansas who were part of the Falls tour. Dave and I walked over to the group and greeted Jack like an old friend.

I stuck my finger in Jack's back like it was a gun and said, "Come on over to the couch, we're going to have a talk."

Jack looked surprised and said, "Okay, just don't shoot me."

The three of us sat on the fancy leather couch with a low glass cocktail table in front of it, I, on one end, Jack in the middle and Dave on the other side of Jack. I asked Jack what he thought he was going to do.

He shrugged and replied, "I'm going to go to Brazil, buy a gun and kill those bad guys. You guys can't stop me. I'm not with the DEA anymore and you don't have any authority over me here in Paraguay."

I said, "Jack, we aren't going to let you do that. You are going to leave Paraguay one way or the other, on your feet or in a box. You are going to leave!"

With that, Jack jumped up screaming "Fuck you!" and went

towards Dave. I jumped up and grabbed Jack from behind, threw a head lock on him with my right arm and started hitting him in the head with my left fist. I was releasing all of my frustrations of the day. Within a minute two big hotel employees with large Colt revolvers were on us. I released Jack and was reaching into my right inside coat pocket for my credentials, when I remembered my S&W Model 39 was in a shoulder holster under my right arm and the Paraguayans might think I was going for it.

I froze, stretched out both my hands in front of me and said, "Dave, show them your credentials and explain who we are and what we are doing." Dave, who carried his pistol on a belt holster, slowly withdrew his credentials from his left inside coat pocket, handed them over to the Paraguayan and calmly explained what was happening and that Randy was inferma in la cabeza (sick in the head).

Things quieted down and after ten minutes two jeeps loaded with police arrived. We, again, explained what had happened and asked the police to contact the Narcotics unit and Carlos. They agreed and then marched us out to the vehicles and carried us to police headquarters, where they literally threw Jack into a cell and awaited the arrival of their commanding officer, who arrived carrying a cavalry sword which was his sign of office.

We again explained what had happened and we all sat there in his dingy office until Carlos and the Narcotics agents arrived. As I didn't want to leave Jack in their jail over night, it was decided that Jack would be taken to Carlos's house with two of the Paraguayan agents and remain there until we determined what we were going to do. I then called Frank in Buenos Aires and told him what had gone down.

Frank said, "Have Carlos bring Jack to Buenos Aires tomorrow and we will have John, who worked with Jack in Los Angeles, meet them at the airport. Then we will handle it from here."

"Oh" I said "There is only one thing wrong. The Paraguayan national soccer team is playing Argentina on Sunday in BA and all flights are booked solid."

Frank laughed and said, "I'm sure you can handle it."

We explained to the Commander of the Paraguayan Narcotics unit what was necessary and he said "No problema, I will take care of it."

So, there it was 11 o'clock and I would have to be up early in the morning to get everything set up. Boy, all I wanted to do was go home, have a stiff drink and crash.

Chapter 26

Jack Is Back. The Other Side Of The Story

While I was separating the things to be shipped from those for sale, I yelled, "What is a good day for the sale?"

From the back room where he was busy packing his shot gun, rifles and several pistols he shouted, "I think Friday would be good. I can get home at noon and help with the end of the sale. Vickie and her sister will be here to help get the sale started."

After two and a half years our tour in Paraguay was near an end. The family had experienced high adventures both enjoyable and exasperating. We had seen the world not as many Americans see the world from their armchairs or sofas but through our own eyes. The children had learned more history and social studies in two years than money could pay for.

All diplomatic service families that left Asuncion for another tour of duty would have a household sale. This saved the chore of packing and the locals and those living on the economy looked forward to these sales. They had little access to the wash and wear clothes, modern kitchen ware and appliances such as blenders, radios, hi-fis and TVs.

The cars the diplomatic community imported were the most sought after items at these sales. Getting a car into Paraguay was difficult, or nearly impossible, and there was a tax on all automobiles that actually doubled the price for the natives. A used car could be sold for the original price paid for it in the states.

We put up flyers at the embassy and the church, sent some to the American school and called all our missionary friends to spread the word.

The sale day arrived. At 7:30 AM the children left for school in the little van which usually picked them up and Gordon left for work at 9:00 AM. The maids and I prepared for the sale. If needed, Vickie would be the translator and her sister would pack and carry heavy items. The sale was to start at 10:00 AM. In Paraguay no one arrives before ten, unlike in the United States, buyers come knocking at your door at 6:00 AM to beat everyone to the goodies.

Everything went smoothly until noon when the children were unexpectedly delivered to the house by the school principal, a personal friend of the family, and an armed guard arrived at the same time to man the front gate.

I tensed at the sight of the children and grew more upset when I saw the armed guard. "What in the world is going on?" I asked.

The principal quickly said, "I received a call from the embassy. Gordon's former partner who was sent home a few months back for medical treatment has returned. He went to Gordon's office looking for his gun. He has left the embassy and is on the streets. Because he would recognize the kids, security felt it was safer for me to bring them home then have them standing by the street waiting for the bus."

As the principal finished explaining all this, the telephone rang. It was the marine guard calling.

"Jack is back. I sent the guard to the house to make sure Jack would not come into the house looking for his gun."

Prior to Jack's transfer home on medical leave, he believed the bad guys were after him and calling him at night. Gordon had taken his gun from him before he left.

By now I was becoming anxious, as my mind churned with what could be happening. I said, "Thank you. Do you know where Gordon is?"

"No, I guess he is in downtown Asuncion somewhere looking for Jack. He was in the office when Jack arrived."

Well all the bases were covered. The children were safe at home and Gordon was after the bad guy. There was nothing I could do but go on with the household sale.

The children were having a fun time helping with the sale, greeting all the shoppers and keeping an eye on the guard. However, now it was more complicated. Everyone who came to the gate had to be checked out by the guard and I had to okay their entry. It really got to be a circus.

The day came to an end and most of the items had been sold. I had not heard anything since noon. Now I began to worry. Somehow with Gordon's job I never worried until night time, especially past 2:00 AM.

The guard remained on the gate and the house was closed up for the night. The moon was high, dogs barked in the distance and the temperature was cool.

It was 9:30 PM and night had fallen. Things were quiet in the neighborhood and I began to pace from window to window. I had no idea what could be happening. I picked up a book and tried to read.

It was 11:30 when the guard clattered his night stick across the gate to gain my attention. At the gate was a tall man with a mustache and a cap on his head, shoulders hunched over intently talking to the guard.

It could be Jack. He had the same build and had a mustache. Even though there was a street light on the corner, I could not see him clearly because they were standing in the shadow of the wall.

The chills ran up my spine. *Had Jack come to the house this late at night? What was I to do if it was him? Gordon had packed up all of his spare guns!*

I slowly opened the door to see the man more clearly when I heard Gordon with a raised voice angrily arguing with the guard, "Yo soy El Patrone de la casa."

On seeing me he yelled, "Tell this son of a bitch who I am!"

The guard turned to me for an approving nod as he had done for many others throughout the day. As I stepped out the door to tell the guard this one was okay, my weird sense of humor kicked in. With a wry smile, I coyly said, "Oh, I don't know that I should do that."

At that Gordon spit out a few choice words which can't be printed here or the book would be censored, the guard opened the gate and slowly walked away shaking his head about these crazy gringos.

Epilogue One

After two years of high adventure we headed home to the good old U.S. of A. This tour of foreign duty had been an education for all of us. The family found out how the rest of the world lived. The differences in their social structure, traditions, religious leanings, food preferences, and government rules made us really appreciate the United States.

What I noticed most about our children was they did not ask for inconsequential things like the others of their age. Greg and Jo had seen what need really was all about. Poor people in foreign countries didn't have indoor plumbing, glass in their windows, shoes on their feet and mandioca, a starchy root, was their main diet.

The first six months in school were difficult for them.

When asked "Where did ya move from?"

They would answer, "Paraguay."

"What did you do there?"

"Our father worked for the embassy. We lived in a big house with a swimming pool; we went fishing for Eldorado, and went down town on a trolley. We took a trip to a ranch and went to the beach where the water was ice cold."

"That can't be true. You are liars. You made that up. Where is Paraguay anyway?"

Needless to say after a few confrontations like this, they no long answered these questions truthfully but made up a good story.

I was happy to get back and settle in Savannah. It was January when we arrive and we took the first few months to look for a house and do Savannah like tourists. The first month we lived on Tybee Beach; the winter was mild and the children enjoyed swimming in the warmer waters of North America.

Being an RN it did not take long to find a job and get back into the routine. With Gordon working many hours setting up the DEA office in Savannah, I set about developing my own life. Taking care of the family came first and then came my job as an RN at St. Joseph's Hospital. Since I had never had a chance to go to college, I also signed up at Armstrong State College to take courses on social work.

My days were full as the family moved forward in this scenario called life.

Epilogue Two

In early December 1973 we were on our way back to the United States and to my new assignment in Savannah, GA, where I was to open the new office of the Drug Enforcement Administration (DEA) as the Agent in Charge.

The marijuana problem had gotten out of control. Boat loads of the drug were being smuggled from Mexico, Columbia and Jamaica into coastal areas of the East, from Louisiana around Florida and up the Atlantic coast all the way to New England.

The disappointments and conflicts of my tour in Asuncion took a back seat in my mind to the challenges of opening the new office and getting the family settled.

It wasn't until several months later, while attending a Regional meeting, where I met one of my counterparts. Joe Garner had just returned from South America and he asked me how I felt about what was happening in our foreign enforcement efforts.

I told him, "That's funny, I really haven't had much time to think about it, but now that you ask, I think it sucks."

He laughed, "Yeah, a lot of us think about it that way. Lots of good press for the State Department and Justice, but really just all smoke and mirrors. What got your ass canned?"

"Well, I had a little disagreement with the Ambassador and the country team because one of my CIs had been picked up and was being tortured by the Federales.

I wanted to make an issue about it and report it to DC, and do a full court press. But the Ambassador ordered me not to make any waves or even report the incident. He mumbled that as he had just sent in a report stating how great the cooperation with the locals had been and any negative report I made would make him and the Embassy look bad and he wasn't going to let a minor incident like this knock his career off track. Screw the CI. He was just collateral damage."

"Really?"

"Yeah, I guess you could say that I was PNGed by my own

Ambassador for doing what I thought was the righteous thing to do. You know, you have to have integrity for the job and more importantly for yourself. I may have screwed up my career, but I can look at myself in the mirror and not feel ashamed; and I managed to get the CI out of jail with only a few cuts and bruises."

"You're 100 percent spot on. To hell with our mission, just make sure the Ambassador looks good and don't get crosswise with the Christians."

"Don't tell me you had a similar experience?"

Joe went on to say, "Not like yours, mine was over some administrative bullshit. The Embassy was stiffing DEA for extra money and expenses that we really didn't spend and I objected. But the Ambassador had signed off on the billing and it would have made him look bad to have to resubmit the paperwork. Real chicken shit, but it was important to him. So, here I am, like you a one tour and done."

"You mentioned the Christians In Action; I never had any problems with them. In fact they were pretty cooperative up until the bit with the CI. Come to think of it though, the Paraguayan Deputy Attorney General who ran the drug enforcement was a source for the Chief of Station. Maybe that had something to do with it."

"Well, you know the government in Nicaragua is Communist and in Honduras and Guatemala the Christians were doing a lot of things to support the right wing contras with guns, supplies, money, and all that kind of shit to overthrow the Commies. In fact the Christians had some 'Cuban' advisors helping with the training. Hell, the Christians had more people, overt and covert, than the rest of the whole Embassy."

I told him, "One of my drinking buddies had the title of 2nd Secretary for Public Works under the Economics section. He never would let on as to what he was really doing, but the only work I ever saw him doing was updating a three year old report on banana production. But, he did make frequent field trips out into the weeds in his special carry-all. It had armor plating, bullet proof windows, self sealing tires, and a special armored gas tank. One night when we were drinking, he bragged that his set of wheels could take a direct hit from anything lighter than a .50 caliber and not even flinch."

It must have been costing a big bunch of money to run operations like that. I wondered what kind of budget they had."

Joe answered, "Ha, that's the other thing. We would get information that the Cubes were running loads of cocaine north and everything would be looking good right up to the last second and then the whole investigation would turn into a puff of smoke. We would go back to the CIs to find out what went wrong and they would just shrug and say it went bad."

"Well, we both know the Agency reads all of our cable traffic. Hell, they run the Comm offices for the whole Embassy. There isn't any way to get around them, unless you send it by a written report through the diplomatic pouch, and in my case even that wouldn't be secret. My secretary's husband was a communicator.

Besides, I think they used to pull the typewriter ribbons and read them. Plus, they had copies of all the combinations to the safes, so there wasn't any place to really hide anything. Shit, after all, they are our intelligence agency and they are damn good at what they do.

Are you saying the Agency is trafficking in drugs to get money to support their activities?"

The Iran Contra Scandal came to light in 1986

GLOSSARY

Amoebas - Amoebiasis, infection of the large intestine caused by a parasite

A/C - Air Craft

ATF/BATF - Alcohol, Tobacco and Firearms/ Bureau of Alcohol, Tobacco and Firearms

AIC - Agent In Charge

AID - Agency for International Development

ASAP - As soon as possible

Attaché - Chief of section in Embassy

Bien Vinedo - Welcome reception - usually a big formal party

BNDD - Bureau of Narcotics and Dangerous Drugs

Carnet - Diplomatic Identification Card issued by Paraguayan authorities

Café doble - Espresso, a strong local coffee

Chaco - The wilderness and desert of North West Paraguay and Bolivia

Christians In Action - CIA

CIA - Central Intelligence Agency

Coke - Cocaine

Comm office - Communications office

DEA - Drug Enforcement Administration

Dulce - Sweet Roll

FBN - Federal Bureau of Narcotics

GTR - Government Travel Request

Happy Hour - Friday night social event, usually at the Marine House

Harvey Wallbanger - A bar drink made with Galliano, fresh squeezed orange juice and vodka on ice with a squeeze of lime.

Kilo - Kilogram 2.2 lbs

Klick- Kilometer, 0.6 mile

LAB - Lloyd Aerolineas Boliviano, Bolivian national airline

LAP - Lloyd Aerolineas Paraguaya, Paraguayan national airline

Lapocho - Tropical forest tree noted for hardness & durability, up to 100 feet high

Mandioca - Local potato type root similar to Taro root

Marine House - Residence for Marine Guards, usually on Embassy grounds

MIL Group - Military Assistance Group

Med Evac - Emergency Medical Evacuation back to US

Mordida - Bribe money

Narc - Federal Narcotics Agent

OAF - Official Advance Funds, money received to be used for official travel or other authorized expenses

On the Job - slang used to advise police you were working U/C (undercover) or plainclothes

PJC - Pedro Juan Caballero, a town on the Paraguay/Brazil border

PNG - Persona non Grata

Post #1- Marine Guard post, usually at the front entrance to an Embassy

RAIC - Resident Agent In Charge

RD - Regional Director

SAIC - Special Agent In Charge, usually of a larger office

Six by six - 6 by 6 is a large military 2 1/2 ton cargo truck

Snitch - Informant, usually cooperating to reduce pending charges against him/her by a police agency but sometimes is a voluntary citizen

Super Tienda - a local store, usually with a dirt floor and no doors and windows

Suits - The bosses

TEA - Treasury Enforcement Agency

U. S. Ambassadors to Paraguay

J. Raymond Ylitalo 8/14/1969 - 9/11/72

George W. Landau 10/13/72 - 10/14/1977

VOR - VHF Omni directional Range, directional beacon at airports, before air traffic control centers and approach radar controls came into being

Family In Paraguay

Made in the USA
Charleston, SC
13 February 2015